COLLABORATIVE
COMMONWEALTH

Robert A. Needham, JD

Title: COLLABORATIVE COMMONWEALTH™

Author: Robert A. Needham, JD

ISBN: **978-1501093845**

Cover Design: Derek Leavitt

Printed in the United States of America

Copyright ©2014 Robert A. Needham, JD All Rights Reserved

DEDICATION

This book is dedicated to my heavenly father who's desire is that all His children (a remnant) to know Him and to be apart of His family.

To my wife, Cheryl-Ann who supports my commitment to bring new thoughts forward and loves me still.

To my friends and business associates who have encouraged me to write this my 15th book, to get his message out, and to hold true to my Purpose of Prospering Others.

Acknowledgements

I want to thank my friends and associates who helped me by reading this book and ensuring this message was accurately translated into this work. They are:

Kathy Roberton	CEO, Cardiff International
Daniel Thomson	Chairman, Cardiff International
Alex H. Cunningham	CEO, FranCnsult
Dr. Tony Dale	Physician, Founder, Sedera Health
Dan Robles	PE, Director of Ingenesist Project
Art & Anita Hall	Retired Executives/Entrepreneurs
Teresa McBride	CEO, McBride and Company
Joey D. Edge	Founder, CEO, The Edge Companies
Jamie Brandenburg	COO, Makeway Wellness
Jeri & Lisa D'Orazio	Living Waters Ranch
Larry Tyler	CEO, Up Your Business
Dr. Mani Skaria	CEO, US Citrus
Dr. Terry Warren	CEO, Warren and Associates
Christopher W. James	Minister
Neil F. Garfield, JD	Lawyer, Author, Blogger
Steve Chelette	CEO, Aligned Convergence
Patrick Kucera	CEO & Entrepreneurial Evangelist
Henrik Jensen	COO, The JetStream Network
Jason Levy	EVP, Founder Magnum Reality
Dan Lahey	Consultant
Cheryl-Ann Needham	Founder, Global Stewards Initiative

TABLE OF CONTENTS

Author's Introduction

To Collaborative Commonwealth™

As I began to frame the chapters of this book, I could not help but sense destiny on the rise. Surely this must have been how our founding fathers felt as they began to craft the elements our United States governance – the U.S. Constitution and the Bill of Rights. Certainly, it is how the drafters of Social Contract Theory such as Plato, Hugo Grotius, Thomas Hobbs, John Locke, Jean-Jacques Rousseau and Pierre-Joseph Proudhon must have felt as they were challenged at every step along the way. Even creditable economists such as Adam Smith (the father of modern economics), Alfred Mitchell Innes, Maynard Keyes, Hernando De Soto, and Harry S. Dent, Jr. who have made predictions or revealed unpopular trends must have shared this same feeling when writing about coming change.

Understanding Collaborative Commonwealth™
George Santayana said, "Those who fail to learn from history, are condemned to repeat it." It is well documented by historians like Alexander Tytler, that in history there are cycles of about 250 years in length in which we "cycle power from the hands of a few to the hands of many." Another view might be, "power from top down to power from the bottom up." These cycles have occurred either through revolution or reformation, as we fought for or against *someone to watch over us!*

During the cycle of power for *kings* and *monarchs* in the 1700's, globally there were individuals seeking to change from tyranny to independence. This gave rise to two of many *isms*:

1) Capitalism and
2) Socialism,

and they are polar opposites. There are many derivatives of thought as to the meaning of each economic system or *ism*.

Extremes and Commons. If you use a continuous line to analyze issues, at each end lie the extreme pro and con and in the middle is the balance or what is often called *the Commons*.

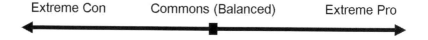

For this book, knowing there are many shades of grey between an extreme pro and an extreme con, I have chosen to often express my opinion from the extreme ends or the Commons (balanced) center for emphasis. There are many additional view points between the extremes, but they are beyond the scope of this book.

Capitalism.   Capitalism is an economic system where the production and the marketplace are controlled by private owners who are in the business of making a profit. I don't find a problem with making a profit, do you? After feudalism (kings and monarchs), capitalism became the favored economic system of the western world.

Adam Smith is credited as the father of capitalism and of economics; his theories and concepts together with others like Ayn Rand and Milton Friedman have laid the foundation of capitalism as we know it today. **Capitalism promotes freedom in the markets and seeks to minimize government intervention in the marketplace.** I agree with this concept.

Today, more than ever, traditional capitalism is under attack from corporate governance advocates. The Harvard Law School Forum On Corporate Governance and Financial Regulation, in a 2009 article entitled "U.S. Corporate Governance Today: A Reshaping of Capitalism," states, "We are in the midst of a true revolution in our private enterprise economic system, much of which is being driven in the name of 'corporate governance' by multiple parties with an ever-expanding agenda (Author: Peter Atkins, blog, 2nd paragraph insert). Basically, capitalism has grown up to have many issues (extremes) and is under constant attack by consumer advocates. I have been a capitalist all my life, but even I recognize something has to change. I call it a reformation where we move away from the extremes, where we disagree; to the Commons, where the majority agrees. This form of governance will require servant leadership as opposed to a dictatorial leadership style. Collaboratism based in sharing will replace traditional capitalism based in scarcity in the extreme.

> **Aspects of capitalism you need to remember when reading this book are:**
>
> - Capitalism is centered on the accumulation of wealth. By its very nature it promotes *self interest.*
>
> - Capitalism is at its best when *scarcity* is at its highest. It functions under the law of supply and demand; with a low supply the price is driven higher and thus creates more profit for those who create scarcity.
>
> - Capitalism works best as a top-down, vertically integrated system which minimizes small entrepreneur business opportunity which is the backbone of our economy.

Socialism. Socialism is an economic system based on the precept of *production for use,* meaning the production of goods and services to satisfy economic demand. Products and services are valued based on their utility to meet human needs as opposed to capitalism where they are based on accumulation of capital and profit. **(You will want to form an opinion on how sharing works within capitalism and socialism.)**

Karl Marx (and lesser Friedrich Engels) is credited often as the father of socialism. Shortly after the French Revolution, socialism had its prominent rise. Marx is also known for his work in the development of communism. However, communism has never reached its purest intent where society is not controlled by government. More often a dictator establishes the state agenda instead of the people.

> **Aspects of socialism (and communism) you need to remember when reading this book are:**
>
> ▪Socialism is centered on the *distribution of wealth,* contrasting with capitalism's *accumulation of wealth.*
>
> ▪Socialism is driven by an economic concept of *free or entitlement* as contrasted with capitalism's economic concept scarcity for increased profit.
>
> ▪Socialism is horizontally integrated and everyone is said to be equal. Socialism rises on the failure of capitalism, and communism is its endgame. Capitalism's concept of individual ownership and rights is replaced with common or state ownership rights in socialism.

Collaboratism, is it the Future?

In every great movement, there is a *remnant* emerging from the best practices from the past. A remnant is defined as the part of something that is remaining when the other part is gone. In religious terms, it is the group that returns or remains after a catastrophe to occupy the *Promised Land.*

In this book, *Collaborative Commonwealth,* I seek establish a movement, a reformation, not a revolution, that remembers and restores the remnant, to the common and not the extreme, of the predominant economic systems (capitalism, socialism, and communism. In the 20th century alone, each of these systems have failed on their own, but with the best parts of each combined together what could they produce?

Collaboration can be defined as *working together* to complete a task, achieving a *shared* goal, or reaching an identical objective with others. Most collaboration requires leadership, which may be social within a decentralized or equalitarian group, and that leadership seeks to capitalize on the tangible and intangible assets within the group.

My good friend, Neil F. Garfield, MBA, JD, an accomplished lawyer, author, visionary, consumer advocate, businessman and blogger (www.livinglies.com) says it this way, "Conservatives conserve nothing and Liberals have liberated no one!" I say, "The fear of loss is greater than the desire for gain." That is why people hold on to the past, they fear the future so much. Another blogger, author, and consultant, Steve Frazee, in a recent blog entitled, Collaboratism: Human-Centered Commerce says,

> My stance that we can improve and transcend capitalism is usually well received, but folks who are on vigilant guard against anything that sounds like socialism can get confused by the language. **Collaboratism is not socialism.** It is not based on social ownership. It continues to leverage the private ownership of capitalism, but rewards owners with economic profits who best provide for human outcomes. Those that do good, do well (emphasis added).

This blog quote gives rise to the concept of pro-rata (proportioned) profit sharing, based on private ownership which has its roots in the Cooperative Movement and not social ownership which is based in socialism.

The remnant is just that, "It provides hopefully the essence (good) of the past with the promises of the future!"

In the 21st century, there is going to be a change. Change is constant and inevitable. Technology has made it possible to communicate globally at the speed of light. Change comes quicker now than it did in the past because of technological advances such as the Internet, digital imagery, and the smart phone. The smart phone and its cousin the smart tablet are as connected to us today as our arms and legs. As I fly on business, I cannot go anywhere that I don't see nearly everyone face down looking at their electronic limb. It is simply how we connect today.

> **Collaboratism is quite different from Capitalism or Socialism (Communism); here are the aspects you should remember for this book:**
> - Collaboratism is centered on *pro-rata sharing* of wealth by producers in the creation of an EcoSystem or EcoSphere.
>
> - Collaboratism comes from a *share* mindset, not scarcity as in capitalism or free as in socialism.
>
> - Collaboratism is *circularly integrated.* All are treated equally from the center (or the Commons), but each is rewarded (valued) pro-rata according to their contribution of time, talent, and treasure.

Collaborative Commonwealth™ as a governance model and Collaboratism an economic system combine to form a remnant of all the good from past systems combined with technology

that makes *sharing* **(in the Commons)** *more feasible today than the extremes of scarcity or entitlement."*

As you read this book, it is in three sections:

1. This Introduction to Collaborative Commonwealth™.
2. The first 11 chapters of the book itself, each with its own Thought Mastery section at the end.
3. Chapter 12, *Thought Mastery* is a quick reference to all the ideas and thoughts that are to be considered when you are learning about Collaborative Commonwealth™.

Lastly, before we begin, this book builds one line upon another and one chapter upon another; I have purposely kept the book short so that it will be a quick read and can be passed to a friend. Attempting to speed read it or skip around is a mistake – you will miss these important concepts.

It is dense; there is not a lot of fluff. It starts with you, a *Drop* in the universe; it demonstrates why leadership is important and how you as a leader are called to a *purpose*; it uncovers this new concept of Collaborative Commonwealth™; it show how to implement this new remnant governance today; and lastly what steps you can take to become involved in this movement.

I recommend getting a notebook to journal as you continue reading this book. I will often ask questions, you should write them in your journal along with your answers. At the end of

each chapter there is a section called, Thought Mastery. I suggest you journal your thoughts at the end of each chapter, as well as your thoughts, during your reading.

The world is changing; will you be a change agent?

Dr. Robert A. Needham

CHAPTER 1 – THE CONCEPT OF WATER

Water in its natural state is a liquid; it is ever changing, when heated it becomes steam (vapor) and when cooled it becomes ice (a solid). Water covers over 70% of the Earth's surface and is vital for the existence of all forms of life, yet less than 3% of water is in its consumable form and 98% of that is either ice or underground. About 96% of the planet's water is in the salty seas and oceans.

Water is important to life, industry, food, recreation, and energy. It is considered the universal solvent. There is no man-made or natural obstacle that water cannot overcome through time, erosion, pressure, or change of state.

Water is fluid; I call it "agile." It can change direction quickly, it can separate and rejoin without loss; it can change with its environment; it is *collaborative* by nature.

Water best describes the new dimension of social contract theory, Collaborative Commonwealth™ and how it will change the way the world governs; reforms society; conducts commerce; organizes businesses, networks, systems, and structures. To that end let's view society through some of water's natural forms: Drops, Streams, Rivers, and Oceans.

Drops

The essence of any great Ocean, River, or Stream begins with one Drop. Drops come in all sizes, shapes, and forms; just like people. Each unique drop of water was created for a purpose, and so were you. This purpose will change throughout the life of a Drop, this is called *Emergence* (see chapter 2); and like you, water can be used over and over again to cause its environment to flourish, change, evolve, and renew without changing the Drop.

In the order of things, drops, like individuals, are uniquely important. They are the building blocks of direction and power, and can define continents. Drops for all their strength are influenced by external forces such as pressure, wind, heat, and cold. In the world today, people, much like drops, must find a way to overcome external forces such as government, economy, debt, jobs, and more. These distractions often affect our relationships with others (Drops) at every level – faith, family, friends, and foes.

It is said that one bad drop, depending on its contents, can contaminate an entire body of water. This is true for people as well. Often it only takes one dissenting or corrupt thought and an entire group of people will sour on what was a clean body of water (thought) before. Politics, religion, business, and any other form of power and influence can change the future by way of introducing a contaminating thought into a once purer form of thought. We will study this later in the book. We will learn how to filter thoughts (make decisions) so that we can clean our dirty water and restore the individuality of each citizen (Drop).

Streams

Since a Drop represents a person, idea, thought, or ideal, a Stream represents an *alignment* of Drops. When one Drop connects with another Drop the impact, influence, or size increases.

I am sure at some time in your life you have watched raindrops form on the hood of a car. The slightest influence will induce movement, and the collision causes even bigger drops to collide with others, rushing head long into others until a stream forms.

Streams are the first form of collaboration among Drops. As they join together and head off in a particular *direction*, they will have influence on the environment around them. Streams continue to swell until a natural flow is established as all the converging drops align with the stream to head in the same direction.

If there is a rock or obstacle in the way, the stream will flow around it, erode it, flow over it, or flow under it; but it rarely is dammed by such an obstacle. Eventually the collaboration of drops will overcome and move past an obstacle once the stream is sufficient in size.

The same is true for people, when they find like-thinking people who possess the same ideals; they tend to congregate in an organization, club, church, on Facebook®, or in a social group. Their agenda (flow) will take these unique individuals (Drops) into a common direction (Stream).

In the 21st century, social media has been a great source of Stream activity. As we explore Collaborative Commonwealth™ more, I am sure you will see the emergence of social media and collaboration in a future marketplace. Each time this Stream changes direction and the flow opens up, new opportunities (marketplaces) emerge.

Rivers

Rivers are merged Streams. When one Stream with its own unique flow finds another Stream and they collaborate by merging into a new mutual direction, *power* is created in the form of a new River. If you think about people, the Streams flow and often form alliances that eventually become a *movement*. Genuine movements affect change; consider the impact on society of movements such as Women's Suffrage, Gay Rights, Civil Rights, and Just Say No To Drugs!

Learning from nature; a properly constructed collaboration of Drops, can promote individual value and rights. It provides a clear direction for governance and allows for the independence of each of the underlying Streams or Rivers to move in their own new direction. The use of technology will generate potential for new opportunities without devaluing each individual Drop and in fact multiplying its unique collaborative value.

Oceans and Other Bodies of Water

If you can find a way to dam up a stream or river, you can create a body of water, like a pond or lake. Creation of a lake is *gathering potential* (more power). This results in new *Ecosystems* being created. The ocean is one of the planet's most valuable resources. For example, oceans yield to fishermen over 200 billion pounds of seafood per year. As a transportation method, oceans are involved with most of the world's goods and services. Oceans are a source of recreation, minerals, and oil. Oceans regulate climate and provide organisms for fighting disease. Oceans offer an almost unlimited source of potential; they are a true and complete Ecosystem.

Whole new industries can spring up around a new pond or lake as people fish, ski, build homes or otherwise use this *collaborative potential of aligned drops.* For people, this new body of water is a reservoir of collaborative knowledge to help others to see the potential power when Drops are gathered together.

Channeled properly, flowing water can generate by-products such as hydro-electrical power without changing the drops in the body of water. In chapter 4, we will see how this idea of *Multiplication* can create multiple opportunities without impacting the nature of the Stream, River, or Ocean that has "collaborated" with the Drops.

A classic example of this concept of society functioning like water is demonstrated by one of the most popular TV shows in the fall of 2013, *Duck Dynasty*. The patriarch of the family, Phil Robertson met Miss Kay and married her about 48 years ago. In the early part of their marriage (alignment or Stream), Phil struggled to provide a basic living and accomplished very little in the way of wealth building; but he was able to interact with his environment and gather food like animals, fish, and plants in the woods (Note: at the end of every show, Phil prays, gives thanks and expresses his gratitude to his Creator for this provision provided without his having to pay for it—a secret to his prosperity—he is thankful and gives honor).

One of Phil's favorite pastimes is duck hunting. Using his unique thoughts and God-given talents, Phil invents an excellent duck call, and he and Miss Kay also produce five sons.

Each of their sons ultimately breaks away from Phil's Stream and starts their own family. The success of Phil's duck call catches on, as other like-thinking duck hunters purchase from Phil his intellectual property (made from natural resources and Phil's intangible assets) which multiplies his value (wealth).

As the kids grow up, Phil and Miss Kay's prosperity enables them to acquire thousands of acres of woods and retire to let the kids run the family business. This allows Phil to enjoy his original passion, loving and living off God's Creation. The merged Streams (his children's families), now a River, and form a company called Duck Commander. As the company continues to prosper (be multiplied), they collaborated to start a TV show as a derivative of Phil's original duck call idea.

The TV show (the second marketplace) becomes such a hit that it becomes a *brand* in and of itself (and a third marketplace emerges). Now each item of the collective intangible intellectual property, including Uncle Si's favorite blue plastic tea glass, is desired by the nearly 11 million Drops (viewers) influenced by the TV show. The result is a movement and a social culture. An Ocean is formed as this River combines with other Rivers (product manufacturers).

Completing the Duck Dynasty example, now an infinite set of markets are multiplied and a host of products are *branded* with their images from band-aides to clothing. Untold millions are now being earned from the *one idea* that became a duck call. Thousands of jobs have been created as each item is licensed, manufactured, and sold through major retailers worldwide. **The intangible has now become very tangible.**

When Rivers merge, all that power becomes a Lake, a Sea, or an Ocean with tremendous potential; and they are truly a force to be reckoned with. Oceans are navigated by Blue Ocean Captains who have the vision to harvest the multiple Rivers of wealth being created by Drops (flowing into) these EcoSystems.

When Phil built the first duck call, I am sure he could not have imagined all the potential in that one idea; but as he merged with other Drops to become Streams, then Rivers, today a true dynasty (a Duck Dynasty) has been created by the Robinson Family Ocean.

Thought Mastery

You are a unique Drop. With whom can you align to form a Stream? Will you become a Stream-Builder? What like interests can make your dreams come true as you merge with others to form Streams and ultimately become a River? Do you have the vision to merge with other Rivers to become your own Ocean? Like Phil Robertson, what is your one BIG Idea?

Remember at each level of collaboration, there are new multiplied marketplaces each one offering an abundance of wealth that can be harvested. Do not rush the process. Take each opportunity as it comes and don't jump ahead of the timing. Build on your sequential successes. **Collaborate more than compete with others and merge your ideas with theirs**.

In the next chapter we will learn about *Leadership Emergence* and how that can impact your future. By the time you fully understand the unique difference between Collaborative Commonwealth™ and the broken capitalistic or socialistic *hierarchal system* (which is failing this planet) you will be armed with the tools to harvest your own success.

In 1843, it was rumored, but untrue, that the US Patent Office recommended shutting down because there were no new inventions left to be created. Just consider the geometric growth since then of ideas (human, intangible, intellectual property). The personal computer is a product of the late 1980's, cell phones a product of the 1990's, the worldwide access to the Internet of the early 2000's, and <u>Social Media now in the 2010's.</u> God made a universe where humans (Drops) could *go forth and multiply!*

What are you called or inspired to do? What is your purpose? The best is yet to come if we learn to collaborate the Drops into mighty Oceans which maintain the identity of each Drop and learn to pro-rata share the profits according to one's labor; not hoard them into broken economic and governmental systems based in hierarchical systems of *top down leadership;* but into collaborative systems where we are all *working together for the common good and each is properly rewarded for their contribution.*

COLLABORATIVE COMMONWEALTH

CHAPTER 2 – LEADERSHIP EMERGENCE

If you are like me, I have always believed that I was created for a special purpose. It has always been there in the back of my mind and deep down in my heart to *help others prosper everywhere,* I call this H.O.P.E.

A friend of mine, Kevin W. McCarthy, is the author several books entitled: *The On-Purpose Person, The On-Purpose Business* and others. You can find more about Kevin on his website (on-purpose.com). He is the *On-Purpose®* expert. He says, "Purpose resides in the heart," and I agree. He also says "Vision is in the head, Mission is in the hands and feet, and Values are in the throat and stomach." He symbolizes this in an image he calls your "On-Purpose Pal." McCarthy emphasizes that you need to be able to express your personal purpose in two words, with the first word ending in "-ing" to show action or intent; therefore, mine is **Prospering Others**. What is yours?

McCarthy concludes, "When we've aligned our heart, head and hands with our values, then we are living with integrity." My wife, Cheryl-Ann wrote a phenomenal book in 2012 entitled *Sound Alignment.* She says, "Everyone's DNA is unique and can be played on an instrument; hence we are all a song." She further says, "In our alignment with others our combined songs are a form of worship." I call it, "Stream Theory!"

Leadership Emergence Theory

One of the great teachers in the concept of Leadership Emergence Theory (LET) is Dr. J. Robert Clinton. There are many others, including myself, who have adapted his teachings for their audiences. If you have time, I suggest you get a copy of his work and study if for yourself.

Let's begin with a formula to define LET: $L = f(P, T, R)$

Meaning Leadership Development is equal to (=) a *f*unction of (**P**rocesses throughout, a leader's life**T**ime, and one's **R**esponse patterns). You might ask, what does this all mean and why does it matter?

Your leadership is the sum of People, Processes, and Patterns (the 3P's) in your life that lead to your emergence of the possible **one idea** (calling) that can change the world as you know it. This influence helps define your intangible intellectual property and gives you the authority to lead on that subject.

Clinton's six phases of Leadership Emergence when combined with the 3P's resemble this structure:

1) People
>   Phase 1: Calling
>   Phase 2: Character

2) Processes
>   Phase 3: Coaching
>   Phase 4: Clarity

3) Patterns
>   Phase 5: Convergence
>   Phase 6: Celebration

As we take a look at each of Phases 1 through 6, we will begin inserting questions for you to begin to master this technique. By engaging with your mind and hands, you may be amazed at your outcomes and findings. Write your answers in your journal.

Starting with Phase 1, our **Calling** is a product of events even before our birth. Family traditions, beliefs, station, and environment establish a foundation such that when we are born a potential leader is being formed. Both positive and negative events help form our image. It is our Response with respect to Time that is the calculus of our leadership emergence. As you begin to look at yourself, write down those people that had influence in your family and yourself growing up.

In Phase 2, **Character** is formed. As a leader begins to develop, inner life lessons are learned as one matures from knowledge to understanding and ultimately to wisdom. Character is different from reputation. Character is who you are independent of your environment (i.e. integrity), while reputation is how you are perceived by others in your environment. Record your essential character qualities in your journal.

In Phase 3, **Coaching** continues to form how you will emerge as a leader. This continues throughout your entire life, but most experts agree that the influence in the early stages of life have the greatest impact. Of course there are exceptions, but those who influence you matter. In your journal, write down those individuals that had the most influence on your family first and then on you.

In Phase 4, **Clarity** emerges when we are presented with opportunities to use our gifts and abilities (talents) in real world experiences. Determine the opportunities you have had to lead, who were the people in your life that offered them, at what **Time** in your life, and most importantly, your **Response** to that opportunity. As you journal you will see **Patterns** emerge and see the unseen hand in your life guiding you toward your **Purpose**.

Phase 5 is **Convergence;** you may have one or more of these occur in your lifetime. A Convergence is when all the previous phases come together and your **Role** as a leader emerges with a certainty that is life changing for yourself and those who follow you. This expression of potential is similar to when an Ocean (chapter 1) or EcoSystem forms. Your Convergence will often involve others (where you are likely the leader) who are aligned with your Purpose (calling). Some people have just one major Convergence and other leaders go through several. Neither leader is more or less valuable; it is just what you were called to do and your response to your environment.

In Phase 6, you are allowed to **Celebrate** your accomplishments. You have achieved a level of wisdom, recognition, reputation, and character that afford you the ability to teach, transforms, and transfer what you have learned. This transference enables **Overlapping Leadership**. Dr. John Maxwell in his book *21 Laws of Leadership*, states that, "There is no success without a successor." It is here that you invest in others. Bob Buford, in his book *Half|Time®*, says, "This is when you transition from pursuing success and enter significance." Your halftime is the transition point and often occurs after a Phase 5 event typically in one's late 40's to 50's. Have you had any critical incidents or processes in your life already? If so, these are valuable in helping you define who you are as a leader, write these down in your journal.

A Well Known Children's Story

As I learned about Leadership Emergence and began to journal my own life's patterns, as a Christian, I could see God's sovereign hand in my work. From ages 5 to 10, before I became a Christian, every summer, I would go somewhere to a Vacation Bible School.

What else was a poor kid to do? It was free, they had snacks, it was air conditioned, my parents got free babysitting, and they did fun stuff and told great stories.

One of those stories was the story of Noah's Ark and it always fascinated me. First, how did Noah hear from God? Where did he get his plans to build the Ark? How did God get all those animals to show up? Inquiring minds want to know such things.

When I was trying to explain to my pastor the events of my life, he shared the work of Dr. Clinton and asked me to examine my life in the context of the Six Phases of Leadership Emergence. It was perfect timing. I had just met Bob Buford, and a few months earlier had read Dr. Maxwell's book on leadership. Call it coincidence or Convergence; I too started my own journal and saw those *patterns* emerge and my life as a leader was forever changed.

A few months ago, I was asked by a friend of my wife to help him with some life coaching. With the economic conditions and lack of any good job situations, he was trying to find himself. As I thought about what to say to him, I remembered, the story of Noah. Noah was an ordinary guy with good character and a fair reputation who *believed* he heard from God to build something called an Ark (his Purpose or calling). As he acted on this belief, it caused his reputation to change. Frankly others thought he was nuts and his vision was stupid, because it had never rained. Nevertheless, he applied his intellect and used the resources around him. It took 100 years for his *vision* to become the Ark. So if it takes a while for your vision, purpose, or calling to become reality, be patient and allow time for your leadership to emerge.

Consider that just because Noah was able **in the natural** to build an Ark, it took a partnering with the unseen to get those animals there. We might not get this Convergence thing at first, but had Noah not been faithful and believed, the animals would have showed up and the mission failed because there was no Ark. Had the animals not showed up, Noah would have not needed such a big boat. Had it not rained, neither would it have mattered. It took People, Processes, and Patterns for this to all work out. It took tangible and intangible things to work together. It took **natural and supernatural events**, and it took a Leader to emerge and make it all happen!

Spheres of Influence

In Collaborative Commonwealth™, we seek to start with the smallest unit (an individual or Drop) and build spheres of influence outward from there such as local, state, regional, national and international. This also is how Streams, Rivers and Oceans develop (emerge).

Spheres are similar to circles of influence that maintain a 360-degree view of all the opportunities where your individual intangible intellectual property and leadership can connect with other similar and dissimilar members. If you work as one it is hard to multiply your self (n × 1 = n); however, collaborating with others creates a multiplied effect and can promote unity $(n \times n = n^2)$. This is sometimes called a *movement*.

I recently attended a seminar by Dr. Christena Cleveland, a social psychology professor from Minneapolis who talked about her book entitled, *Hidden Forces That Keep Us Apart*. Dr. Cleveland says, that when seeking collaboration as a leader, we have to be *cognitive generous* and not *cognitive efficient* to avoid entering into an organization state where there becomes an *"us – them division"* by categorizing people to simply save time. We have to be willing to collaborate and *share our brain space* with others and not force them into the image of what we think is right, but seek a mutuality that leads to unity and multiplication.

Recall Noah; as he acted on his Purpose, his reputation was challenged and others called him a nut. I recently had the opportunity to watch a three minute video on TED TALK where Derek Sivers shared a video about *How To Start A Movement*. (www.ted.com/talks/derek_sivers_how_to_start_a_movement). In this video, was a *secret* that you must know if you want to lead (form) a Stream, River, or Ocean (a movement).   Here is a summary of that wisdom:

- A leader needs the guts to stand out and be ridiculed.
- A leader must be easy to follow, duplicate or multiply.
- The first follower has a critical role; he is going to show everyone else how to follow.
- The leader must embrace the first follower as an equal; it is no longer about the leader, but it is about them!

- Movements are not private, they must be public.
- Leaders may get the credit, but the followers transform the *lone nut* into a leader. Cherish your followers; share the limelight and the revenue, if any.

Effective Leadership

There is much commentary on what makes an effective leader. Here are but a few of the characteristics that I have discovered:

- **Lifetime Learners.** Effective leaders are always looking to improve themselves learning new things everyday.
- **Attend Formal Training.** Effective leaders invest in their growth by attending long-term training and education to enhance their leadership skills.
- **Attend Informal Training.** Effective leaders look for seminars and workshops from one hour to several days to enhance their leadership skills and gain perspectives from other leaders.
- **Align Well.** Effective leaders learn how to align themselves with the right mix of team members. Furthermore, they understand that they may only lead for a season, and then follow for a season.
- **Have A Sense Of Destiny.** Effective Leaders know that they are called to be and do something greater than they really are.
- **Add Value To Those They Serve.** Effective leaders are servants and always give more than they take.
- **Pursue Excellence.** Effective leaders want more that to just get it done. They want to get it done well ahead of schedule, under budget, empowering others, and bringing honor to the project.

- **Seek To Make Right Choices.** Effective leaders do not take the path of least resistance; they seek to make the right choice not the easy choice.
- **Character.** Effective leaders develop a moral compass throughout their lifetime.
- **Excellence.** Effective leaders do not command excellence, they build excellence.
- **Integrity.** Effective leaders are undiminished in their moral and ethical principles.
- **Become Stewards.** Effective leaders are able to steward resources of others without jealousy, envy, greed, or desire to take what is not theirs. They are open-handed, not closed handed.
- **Have Discipline and Are Responsible.** Effective leaders do it first. They are not late. They set an example. If something goes wrong, they accept responsibility for it, not find someone to blame.
- **Share With Followers' Pro-rata.** According to followers' investment of time, talent, and treasure make distributions.

Thought Mastery

In your journal, list all the ways you have intentionally or unintentionally begun to emerge as a leader. Then write answers for each of the questions that follow.

- Where are you in your LET Phases?
- Are you now in Convergence?
- What are you doing to establish spheres of influence?
- How have you invested in yourself to become a more effective leader?

- Which characteristics of effective leadership do you have?
- What outside influences could take you to the next level if you approach with an open mind as to what others have to say and offer?
- Are you maximizing your potential?
- Have you found your first followers?
- Do you treat your followers as equals?
- Do you pro-rata share with your followers according to their commitment of time, talent, and treasure.
- Where is your Ocean?
- Are you willing to become a *"Blue Ocean Captain?"*

In the next chapter, we will begin to learn how to govern, control, steward, and manage our calling (Purpose). This is called *"Governance."*

CHAPTER 3 – BUILDING BLOCKS OF THE NEW GOVERNANCE

Governance is *a way to govern, control, steward, or manage.* So when I speak of new governance, I am speaking of a new way to govern, steward, or manage a remnant going forward in parallel to the existing forms of governance, which are all failing.

H. G. Wells, in *The Outline of History* (page 959), said,

> *The true strength of rulers and empires lies not in armies and navies, but in the belief of men that they are inflexibly open and truthful and legal. As soon as government departs from that standard, it ceases to be anything more than* **'the gang in possession'***, and its days are numbered.* (Emphasis added).

Chaos, Order, and Collaboration

To try to understand the dilemmas of the contemporary world, we must investigate the processes of social change in past centuries. The concept of *hegemony* whereby a group or nation is geopolitically controlled (a form of governance) by a leader state (the hegemon) over subordinate states has been with us since antiquity. For example, the city-state of Sparta was the hegemon of the Peloponnesian League (6th – 4th century BC). By the end of the 19th century the British Empire was the hegemon for nearly one-fourth the global population from a small island. In the 20th century the USSR and Germany sought regional hegemony (sphere of control–governance) and ultimately global hegemony during WWII and until the early 1990's.

It is projected that in the 21st century, the United States, called a hegemonic superpower, through its unilateral military and political actions, specifically in the Middle East, is projecting global governance; but is the United States able to sustain that role? The United States, acting as global hegemon, may lead, but will likely fail to sustain this role due to its financial crisis and degraded credit standings. Such was the story of Rome, as they became a world power. Rome over-extended its treasury by having troops in conflicts and outpost all over the known world and by providing entitlements to citizens in an attempt to control the masses. Then, it was welfare and games in the Coliseum. Today, it is welfare and professional sports or reality TV. Will the United States repeat the demise of the Roman Empire?

In the beginning of government, there was **Chaos**, which is a state of total confusion with a lack of organization or order. As discussed earlier, hegemon nation-states have for hundreds of years sought to bring **Order** by subordinating lessor states. This is called a one-up one-down (hierarchal or vertical) governance.

Emerging in the 21st century is a new social contract theory based in **Collaboration**, a remnant form of governance. I call it Collaborative Commonwealth™. The new Collaborative Economy does not subordinate others, but treats others as equals and is more balanced (Commons, open, or circular) in its organization as opposed to vertical hierarchy organization in government or horizontal hierarchy organization in non-profit and social concepts.

Leaders in many nations, including the United States, are calling for a *New World Order*, which is a global hegemon, leading to a one-world leader (a form of monarch or dictator). What are your thoughts? I think it is even more fragile, I think we should think smaller, collaborate, and be more agile!

Dee Hock, the former Founder and CEO of VISA, in his book, *Birth of the Chaordic Age* (page 6), said, "The organization of the future will be the embodiment of community based on **shared purpose calling** to the higher aspirations of people"(Emphasis added). He further said (page 7), "…organization begins with an intensive search for Purpose, and then proceeds to Principles, People and Concept, and only then to Structure and Practice."

Clearly Dee understood the next generation of organizational structure (governance) is based in a non-linear open construct where individuals are free to explore as if anything is possible. They are freed from the traditions of classical organization structure (hierarchy) toward a more open agile style based in the individual *collaborating the group* (Drops, Streams, and Rivers), not the group influencing the individual (traditional one-up one-down). Consider another quote from Dee (page 9),

> *When people set aside all consideration for existing conditions, free themselves to think in accordance with their deepest beliefs, and do not bind their thinking with structure and practices before considering meaning and values, they usually discover that the number and variety of people and entities to participate in governance, ownership, rewards, rights, and obligations are much greater than expected.*

Collaborative Commonwealth™ is such a governance construct. It enables a wide variety of peoples and entities to find a common Purpose and mutual benefit. **This is not socialism where the whole is equally distributed to each participant; rather, it is just the opposite; it is where each is rewarded pro-rata according to their actual contribution of non-tangible and tangible property, time, talent, and treasure.** Before we explore this further, let's add some more thoughts into the mix.

Individual Values and Rights

To understand the dilemmas of the contemporary world, we must investigate the processes of social change over the centuries. I first discussed the "Cycle of Power and Revolution" in my book, *Wealth 3.0 – Saving America One Small Business At A Time* (pages 9-18). These cycles of approximately 250 years are symbolized by **hegemony – revolution – independence** and often turn by innovation. Consider the United States. We left the monarchies of Europe to come to the New World to free ourselves of the tyranny of a monarch; but it took a revolution to achieve our freedom. This was a move from the "power in the hands of a few to the power in the hands of many." Once we were a nation unto ourselves based on **individual values and rights**, a republic form of governance, we evolved through struggle (a civil war) and chose federation versus confederation as our form of unity based on a democratic method as our hegemon (about 1500 to 1750).

However, because of the Industrial Revolution (1750 to 2000), we cycled again and **gave our individual values and rights over to another** form of governance, the capitalistic business organization (the corporation) as our new hegemon. This was the "cycle of power back from the many to a few." Some would argue that I overstate the impact of *big business*; but is our government the government truly of our forefathers, or the government of the lobbyists? Again, I am viewing these traditions **from the extremes** to make a point. Of course there are many shades of grey in the reality of it all.

Today, our government representatives pass laws they have neither read, nor written; and they use *crisis* as their reason for change.

The next revolution, the technology revolution, is bringing about yet another cycle. I predict that we will move once again from the "power of a few to the power of many." This time, because of the Internet and social media, communication is at the speed of light. People are rethinking "who they want to watch over them;" a hegemon or another form, where individual values and rights are not minimized by the plans of a few.

There is clear evidence this new form of governance is emerging and its related economy is being created from a fusion of social media, collaboration, and technology.
Let's explore what it is and what it is not...

Republic not Democracy

Let's now drill down a bit deeper to secure the foundational elements that make Collaborative Commonwealth™ a powerful governance concept. We will view it from the extremes of what it is and what it is not.

A **Republic** is a government in which the supreme power rests in the body of the citizens (the many) who are entitled to vote and whose rights are exercised by representatives chosen directly or indirectly by them. **Any body of persons viewed as a**

Commonwealth or a state in which the head of the government is neither a monarch, nor the *hereditary head* of state (i.e. neither from the Bush or Clinton families).

A **Democracy** is defined as a government by the people; a form of government in which the supreme power is vested in the people and exercised directly by them or by their elected agents under an electoral system.

So what is the difference? It is subtle but essential. In a Republic the power is vested in each citizen; in a Democracy, sovereignty is vested in the majority of the group (hence, a form of hegemon). **A Democracy is a gang in possession!**

Democracies historically exist about 250 years until in the words of Alexander Fraser Tytler (1747 – 1813), later Karl Marx, and others. Cited from *Preserving Democracy* (page 26) Elgin Lewis Hushbeck, et al.

> *A Democracy cannot exist as a permanent form of government. It can only exist until the voters discover that they can vote themselves largesse from the public treasury. From that moment on, the majority always votes for the candidate promising the most benefits from the public treasury with the results that a Democracy collapse over loose fiscal policy; always followed by a dictatorship. The average age of the world's greatest civilizations has been about 200 years. Great nations rise and fall. The people go from bondage to spiritual*

truth, to great courage; from courage to liberty; from liberty to abundance, from abundance to selfishness; from selfishness to complacency from complacency to apathy; from apathy to dependence, from dependence back again to bondage.

My concern is that we will become a dictatorship or a socialist regime. Truthfully a democracy is a dictatorship by a small group if left unchecked by the individuals. If the United States was true to its Constitution crafted by our founders, and operated as a Republic (as it should), then we would not see the passing of laws in the middle of the night or just before a major holiday out of fear or influence by lobbyists or other control groups. Our citizens would be holding these bank robbers accountable for their actions.

The founding fathers of the United States saw the difference between a Republic and a Democracy and other such fine details; consider these excerpts from the Declaration of Independence: "We hold these truths to be self-evident, that all men are created equal, that they are endowed by their Creator with certain unalienable Rights that among these are Life, Liberty and the pursuit of Happiness." And consider these additional words:

That to secure these rights, Governments are instituted among Men, deriving their just powers from the consent of the governed, — That whenever any Form of Government becomes destructive of these ends, it is the Right of the People to alter or to abolish it, and to institute new Government, laying its foundation on such principles and organizing its powers in such form, as to them shall seem most likely to effect their Safety and Happiness.

What does this say to you? I think it is saying that when my value and rights are transferred away from me, as a citizen I have the right to demand a change. In recent years, the law has changed. To suggest such a revolution to overthrow our government is considered an act of terrorism punishable by imprisonment without any civil rights. **This change, I speak of is not by revolution but by reformation of how we as a culture govern our daily lives.** We are allowed to organize as **personal corporations or LLCs** and do as we like. Consider how will you organize to maximize your value and rights in the 21st century? Let's examine some other key differences in how Collaborative Commonwealth™ as a remnant form of governance can bring reformation and recover our destiny.

Confederation not Federation

As we have said, Republics align better with a confederation or league or collaboration and Democracies align better with Federations. The difference is where the *Central Powers* lie. In Federation, the Federal Government is the sovereign and in Confederation the State (or the citizens) is/are the sovereign and the Confederacy is the servant. This ideal closely aligns with the writings of Benjamin Franklin in 1787 (See *Voting In America: A Reference Handbook* (page 206) Robert E. DiClerio).

41

In Collaborative Commonwealth™, the sovereignty must be at the individual level such that each individual has unique value and inalienable rights that are not subject to a sovereign; that the individual *volunteers* to collaborate with a project, group, or government who has aligned interests and serves the needs of its members pro-rata according to each individual's contribution. Now that might make your head hurt the first time you read it, but, the more you think about it, this is the way it should be.

Let's go back to the Drop, Stream, River examples. A Drop is an individual with unique value and inalienable rights (I believe, given by his Creator) which transcends geographic boundaries, birth, or even family. When Drops align (voluntarily) with other Drops they form a Stream. A Stream could be likened to a City or County. When Steams find a method of collaboration, they increase in power and strength and we called them a River. A River could be likened to a State. When Rivers agree to collaborate they form lakes, seas, and for our discussion an Ocean. Oceans are an example of a confederacy of collaborative Rivers, Streams, and most importantly Drops. Here Ocean could be the same as nation.

Let's consider another example. Ten people (Drops) each with a unique talent collaborate together and form a business (Stream). They wish to interact with other Drops and Streams to conduct commerce. Occasionally, two Streams want to merge in order to capture more market, share in a product development, or expand capability. This creates power and more control and becomes a River. However, the River is still made of Drops that are collaborating and each has ownership pro-rata to their contribution to the effort. This is similar to a member of a cooperative who receives a Patronage Refund (dividend) pro-rata to their patronage (use or contribution). What is excellent about this relationship is the producer and consumer can align to establish a local, regional, national, or international marketplaces.

This collaboration may go on only for a season of time; individuals may all participate in a project that is an Ocean but are not always required to do it this way. During that time, however, the Ocean provides a boundary (rules of engagement) so that order (governance) is maintained. There must be order or chaos reigns. **Freedom is not lost in order, it is revealed.**

Reformation not Revolution

Martin Luther wrote the *95 Theses* on church reformation (circa 1517) and changed the religious government of his day. There are others that say this was the birth of capitalism as well. In the 21st century, there is a need for economic and governance reformation in the United States, as well as globally.

As stated before, a revolution in modern times may not provide good legal standing for your movement. A revolution is seen as an overthrow or repudiation and the thorough replacement of an established government or political system by the people governed. Often it requires violence. Clearly this is not collaborative. Also, the Patriot Act and other legislation in the U.S., may have made such activities terrorism and with that comes numerous negative outcomes.

Reformation is the act or process of improving something; or someone by removing; or correcting faults, weaknesses, problems, etc. Everyone wants improvement. Change is however; often resisted, but recently crisis has been publically embraced as the method for change.

Consider telecommunications. Clearly today we have the technology to have cell phones connect via satellite, correct the dropped calls problem, and overcome the lack of tower coverage. Then why don't we? The answer is that cell towers are part of the old paradigm where investments were made in these towers (this is called legacy equipment) and moving to a future technology would impact those investors return on investment (ROI). Here is an example where economic resistance is greater than the impact of future technology even though people suffer from a legacy concept. Scarcity is used to maintain the investor's ROI.

Sharing and the Collaborative Economy

In the 21st century, consumerism is changing also. In the 1990's, social media drew commercial and more importantly non-commercial users to the Internet. Online purchasing, networking, and engagement, according to YCharts.com has grown from $9.4 Billion 4Qtr1999 to $71 Billion 1Qtr2014 with an average annualized growth rate of 20.09%. Facebook, according to Yahoo.com, has over 1.1 Billion subscribers as of March 2013 which represents 1/6th of the global population. This change is having an impact on jobs and brick and mortar retail business that must evolve or die.

Sharing, is the consumer's answer to rising prices and is bringing about **the reformation of retail**. Rather than buy new goods from big brands; consumers are opting to purchase pre-owned goods from each other (i.e. eBay and Amazon). Crowdsourcing is emerging as the reformation of retail continues.

Crowdsourcing is the process of obtaining needed products, services, and intellectual property (IP), by soliciting contributors of the group (Stream, River, Ocean) or EcoSystem using online as the method of connecting and collaborating. Google and venture capitalists are making substantial investments into these initiatives especially if they are also connected to mobile applications. Many of the applications serve what is called the Maker's Movement.

The Maker's Movement is the cottage industry based in hi-tech and includes ideas like robotics, 3-D printing, and sometimes called CNC (computer numerical control) using CAD (computer aided design) and CAM (computer aided manufacturing). Basically, we are doing from home what we used to do only do in factories. This is the **reformation of manufacturing**. In the future, the Framisdortin (see chapter 8) will become an essential element to connect the new economy. I might suggest you read *Makers –*

The New Industrial Revolution by Chris Anderson. Specifically, page 14 "ideas spread when shared" and page 15 "Inventors are freed to be entrepreneurs."

The majority of Sharers today come from the 18 to 35 year old crowd (48%) and are the early adopters; but the age 55+ are catching on quickly as Baby-boomers see Sharing as the way they might overcome the losses incurred during the financial crisis after 2008. Many boomers have had to return to work in order to sustain their lifestyles. Sharing is not a new idea; it is an old idea whose time has come. The first major markets to use sharing are consumer goods, services, transportation, space management (commercial and hospitality), and funding. According to Vision Critical/Crowd Companies, the top nine brands for sharing in the U.S. are: Craigslist, eBay, Amazon, VRBO, FreeCycle, FundingCircle, Kiva, and Kickstarter. Pre-owned goods are the number one category as of January 2014. This is not a new idea; who hasn't bought a pre-owned car or home?

Another study conducted by Vision Critical/Crowd Companies showed the current top 12 shared things, they are: books, cars, clothes, phones and other electronics, furniture, cleaning services, money, toys, and writing services.

Sharing has gone viral as the majority who has tried it, liked it, and is telling all their friends! I believe the ultimate form of sharing will occur as I describe in Chapter 8 – The Framisdortin.

On the other hand, technology has brought about reformation on several levels due to sharing. Some examples are:

- The **publication and printing reformation** has greatly expanded by the creation of e-books, e-zines, and online video.
- The **photo business reformation** has been advanced with digital pictures.
- The **postal service reformation** by email.
- The **music business reformation** by websites like YouTube, Napster, and Vimeo.
- Even **local news reformation** by social media. Many people get their news on Facebook first.

Other industries are feeling the impact of reformation such as advertising, energy, and consumer goods distribution. **The world of consumer goods and services is reforming, why not our government?**

Reformation is how we change. In the next chapter we will look at Evolution to Change.

Thought Mastery

What do you see as the processes of CHANGE going on right now?

Do you understand the concept of hegemony? As our nation, like Rome, deploys its military around the world and continues to increase entitlement programs, do you believe that the United

States will continue to be a global hegemon? If not, what impact will this change have on your way of life in the 21st century?

Collaboration is emerging as a new social contract theory in the 21st century which I propose should use Collaborative Commonwealth™ as its form of governance, creating Collaboratists who believe in pro-rata sharing and caring for their community and nation.

Dee Hock...*"the organization of the future will be the embodiment of community based on a 'shared purpose'... Purpose first, then proceeds to Principles, People, and Concept; and only then to Structure and Practice..."*

There are cycles of approximately 250 years, (hegemony – revolution – independence) which cause *"power to move from the hands of a few to the hands of many"* and back again. The Industrial Revolution took back our power and placed it in the hands of new kings, the capitalist corporations, headed by Imperial CEOs. **We are not saying corporations are bad, but that their governance has to REFORM.**

Collaborative Commonwealth™ is more like:
- A Republic or Commonwealth
- A Confederation
- A Reformation
- Believes in Pro-Rata Sharing and Community Caring

Collaborative Commonwealth™ is NOT:

- A Democracy (headed to Dictatorship)
- A Federation
- A Revolution
- Driven by Scarcity or social concepts of Free or Entitlement.

With Collaborative Commonwealth™ sovereignty is at the individual level allowing voluntary participation in projects and the ability to succeed or withdraw when the plan does not meet their Purpose.

Sharing will play the major role in the emergence of the Collaborative Economy.

Technology has brought reformation (change) in the publication, photography, music, and communication. It will be a major component in how we collaborate and govern in the future.

CHAPTER 4 – EVOLUTION TO CHANGE

The Evolution to Change from a Global Industrial Economy based in *"scarcity"* to a Global Collaborative Economy based in *sharing* consider a social economy (or a polar opposite) based in *entitlement or free.* The following chart depicts the path over time from Industrial through Social to Collaborative Economy.

Industrial Economy	Social Economy	Collaborative Economy
Centered on Accumulation of Wealth (Self)	Centered in Distribution of Wealth (Network)	Centered in Sharing Access to Wealth (EcoSystem or EcoSphere)
Self Centered or Scarcity Mindset	Free or Entitlement Mindset	Pro-Rata Share Mindset
Vertically Integrated Dictator Power At The Top	Horizontally Integrated Democracy Small Group Control	Circularly Integrated Commonwealth Individual Power

We will discuss each economic concept in detail in this chapter.

Capitalism is the polar opposite of Socialism and is at the extremes (pro and con), where Collaboratism is balanced (centered). The chart below shows how various political parties and ideologies have divided this country with the pro and con extremes. Collaborative Commonwealth™ brings into balance all these systems. It seeks unity and not division by drawing the core of all these groups to the center where real reformation and change will take place.

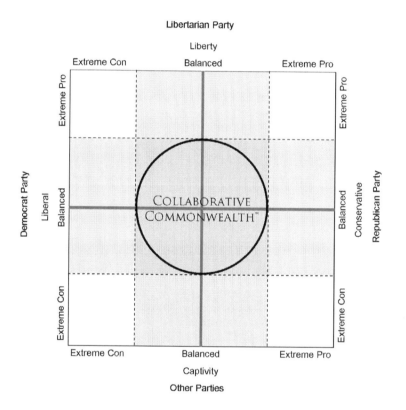

The **grey area is the unity zone** where the groups have the fewest differences. Collaborative Commonwealth™ narrows that by another 50% and finds the central issues where they can hopefully unify and agree. **The circle represents a new structure, which if this movement catches on, could establish a new party to elect a president of the United States as early as 2016 or 2020. A bold but true possibility! Will you join this movement, will you establish this mandate?**

In the 20th century, in the United States, the debate has been conservative versus liberal, Democrat versus Republican, and ownership versus entitlement. The 20th century will go down in history as the *Century of Division.*

In the 21st century we are evolving and change is a necessity. We are learning to grow by sharing and that is why I believe that the 21st century will be known as the *Century of Multiplication* (see Chapter 5 – Collaborative Economics: Multiply not Divide).

Cycles of Economic Change

Continuing our discussion from chapter 3, in "Chapter 1: The Cycle of Power and Revolution" of my book, *Wealth 3.0 – Saving America One Small Business At A Time*, I discussed the cycles of power which have been historically changed by revolution about every 250 years or so. George Santayana, a philosopher, essayist, poet, and novelist (and others) are credited with this quote "those who fail to learn from history are condemned to repeat it."

Looking back, we certainly see these cycles of economic change in the history of the United States. American's desires are for "Life,

Liberty, and the Pursuit of Happiness." Happiness is a journey; it is the pursuit (the journey or emergence) that makes us happy, not the actual attainment. This is why we have always been a people and a nation in favor of change. We fled the tyranny of monarchies where we endured a form of *physical slavery* and where the king owned everything. I call this the Freedom Revolution to gain our independence or Wealth 1.0 – Title to Land. Only in the next 250 years for us to slide into *fiscal slavery*, during the Industrial Revolution (about 1750 to 2000). Here we changed to the rule of "big business" as our monarch, or what I called, Wealth 2.0 – a belief in *percent ownership* controlled by an Imperial CEO (on the extreme). Only to be burdened even more with global debt brought about by fiat money (a currency which derives its value from government regulation, and act of law, or is debt-based). The Technology Revolution (2000 to present), what I called the rise of "small business," created by the agility of technology or Wealth 3.0 – Personal Ownership or the Personal Company.

These 250 year cycles in history have been accurate for about the last 2000 years; but in 1965, Moore's Law (named after Gordon E. Moore – Co-Founder of Intel Corporation), predicted an exponential change within the change (a derivative with respect to time, an accelerator occurred) that the invention of the microprocessor and its evolution would speed up time such that, according to several technologists, Moore's Law may reach its singularity before 2020 requiring yet another technological advance of the microchip technology to advance.

It is during this time, 1965 to about 2020, that our nation has evolved in its *social contract* with the emergence of the other extreme based in this entitlement mindset or dependence on government to provide a quality of life. Certainly, it may have begun with the introduction of Social Security (1935 to 1937), but several major changes began in the 1960s and now the children of the 60's are running the government.

In Chapter 4: Worldly Economics – By Division" in my book *Why Divide When You Can Multiply? Sow A Seed – Feed A Nation*, I look inside the 250 year cycles to the 40 and 80 year cycles, to study the impact of fiat capital. It begs a question, *Have the cycles now shortened?* For example, compare 1955 to 2035 (an 80 year cycle) which is my 40-80 cycle. Note: This chart is for example purposes only and not accurate for forecasting events. It is an example of the concept only. See Chart top of next page.

If you plot the S-curves (both 40 and 80 year life cycles) and look at the impact of population growth (Baby-boomers and Millennials) you will find a convergence that begins around 1995 to 2025 which indicates 1) a crash starting about 2008, 2) a possible further economic crash (Wall Street 2014-15) can be seen with finer detail and 3) an economic recovery starting about 2016 to 2025). Harry S. Dent, Jr., in his book *The Great Depression Ahead – How to Prosper in the Debit Crisis of 2010 – 2012*, predicts we will not see economic recovery until 2023. Coincidence? I think not; the future is more predictable than we think, at least mathematically speaking.

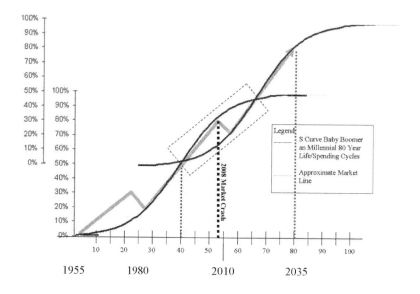

So what does all this mean? First, the 250 year cycles, much like Moore's Law, have been impacted by technology and we should look more at the underlying 40 and 80 year cycles of change that are generational or lifespan driven. Next, we have to observe: 1) the mindset changes from scarcity or hording; 2) to distributed entitlement or free; 3) to what I believe is emerging in the next decade, collaborative sharing. So let's drill down a bit deeper and look at each of the three economic systems: 1) Industrial; 2) Social; and 3) Collaborative.

Elements of the Industrial Economy

Entrepreneur. The entrepreneur, the inventor, and the dreamer are the heroes of the industrial economy. Their ideas created great change the last 250 years. One of the things I have learned however; there is a difference between an *initiator* and an *organizer*. What I mean is that left to their own devices, the inventors would still be tinkering in their garages and labs because they seek perfection of their inventions; where organizers are happy at 80 to 90% perfection and go to market. We see this throughout the last 250 years as inventor's created ideas and industrialists capitalized their ideas into products and services.

Self Centered. The individual entrepreneur and the corporate entity, as industrialists, in the last 250 years, have hoarded their wealth either to themselves, or an elite few at the top of a company. Even so-called public companies have really not shared the wealth with their public shareholders. If you study the modern day stock market, the truth is that share appreciation has little to do with the actual value of the company; but actually in the speculation between a buyer and a seller. The stock market creates winners and losers trading on a stock certificate not really the success or failure of the company. After the initial public offering (IPO), the company does not receive any of the money from a stock trade. That money is between the winners, stock brokers, and the losers only. Now their speculation does increase or decrease the value for the holders of the stock, which often includes the founders of the company; but it does not really add to the company cash itself unless it sells (issues) more stock. Of course that appreciation or depreciation (considering dilution) could help or hurt the company.

Scarcity. A principal in capitalism and its related economics is called *supply and demand*. Basically, it works this way: if an item is scarce, the price goes up and if it is abundant, the price goes down. If my goal is only to make the most margin, that is selling price minus cost of goods; then I want to introduce scarcity and therefore increase my profits. This is niche marketing versus commodity marketing. Any good capitalist knows the money is made by the unit sale in niche marketing versus the sale of units in commodity marketing. To make money in commodity marketing, you must have another factor called *velocity* or high turn of inventory. Not every business can be niche, some require a commodity approach. The more niche, likely the more entrepreneurial and the more commodity, the more industrial by nature. For example Wal-Mart is more like commodity clothing store, where White House Black Market is a niche clothing store.

Vertically Integrated. Sometimes referred to as the supply chain, vertical integration requires that the maker of things seek to capture as much margin as possible from manufacturing to consumption. Often manufacturers, rely on a system of intermediaries (the supply chain) to market their products and services to consumers. They are called brokers, sales people, distributors, jobbers, and ultimately retailers. Each intermediary shares in a portion of the profit margin with the manufacturer. If I seek vertical integration, then I seek to eliminate intermediaries and capture that profit margin.

Dictator Governance. The Imperial CEO has become the poster child of top-down dictator style hierarchical business. Today, more than ever in history, we have one person acting as Chairman, CEO, and President. The concept of corporate governance is almost non-existent – no checks and balances. We even see it in our government as the president of the United States uses structures such as Presidential Directives, Czars, and the like to avoid following the intended governance of the three part system of Executive – Legislative – Judicial (in which our form of government was designed to operate). These leaders, by avoiding good governance, are setting themselves up to be dictators who are self-centered in their goals and objectives.

Elements of the Social Economy

Social Entrepreneur. Someone once asked me, "Is it easier to teach someone to become a millionaire (the traditional entrepreneur) or is it easier to teach someone to become a philanthropist? (A social entrepreneur)" (emphasis added). Being a millionaire is for self and being a philanthropist is about others. Neither is wrong, they are just different. Becoming a millionaire is more of a goal to the entrepreneur, where to a philanthropist it is just a milestone to an ultimate goal.

There is much discussion today on what defines a social entrepreneur. I like this simple definition, social entrepreneurs are looking to create sustainable resources by using innovative hybrid structures: large and small; old and new; religious and secular; in various forms of governance: government, for-profit, non-profit, and cooperative. These entrepreneurs often express their results in terms of social capital. Social capital is valuing of the collaboration of others and their networks for a common goal.

Traditional entrepreneurs are innovative in their business designs too; but measure results in profits and losses. Whereas, social entrepreneurs measure their results in people helped or lives changed.

Network Centered. The social entrepreneur is network centered. Terms like, social media, crowd-sourcing, crowd-funding, tribe, Facebook, etc. describe the community of the social entrepreneur. Social entrepreneurs use technology extremely well. Twitter, YouTube, and similar means of communication have taken the place of face-to-face business. These networks are very *cause sensitive* and ideas such as flash mobs and the Occupy Movement have met with great success. President Obama attributed his use of social media in both his election and re-election and it has now become a standard in political playbooks and social gatherings. Lastly, remember, *People don't care how much you know, until they know how much you care.* Also remember the secret we learned in chapter 2 of the first follower.

Entitlement or Free Mindset. Entitlements, while created to help those who cannot help themselves (a noble cause), they have been so misused that today they make up the majority of the US Budget and the abuse and fraud are unbounded. Alexander F. Tytler in a writing commonly known as the *fatal sequence* and about the rise and fall of democracies said, "Great nations rise and fall. The people go from bondage (monarchies) to spiritual truth (Reformation), to great courage (the Pilgrims), from courage to liberty (the American Revolution), from liberty to abundance (the Industrial Revolution), from abundance to selfishness (Imperial CEO, Wall Street, etc.), selfishness to complacency (employee mindset), from complacency to apathy (entitlements), from apathy to dependence (let the government watch over me) from dependence to bondage (a dictatorship)" (emphasis added). You would have thought he was a prophet to the rise and fall of the United States, Europe, and other industrialized nations.

Give-away, entitlement, and free mindsets are leading us to social decline, not happiness. I am for taking care of the poor (the real poor widows, orphans, and the infirm). We need the efforts of social consciousness; it is the human thing and the right thing to do. We need to do it ourselves and not leave it to a government. Wouldn't you agree? I think charity should be kept local where the need can be seen and managed. However, the current government strategy is more socialist and unsustainable.

Horizontally Integrated. In business, horizontally integrated means that you seek to capture like or similar products and eliminate competition. Horizontal Integration provides for real leverage, but can lead to a monopoly or even anti-trust issues. This is one of the reasons that the Cooperative Movement has advanced in the last decade. Cooperatives (CoOp) from the beginning have been granted exemptions to the law especially in the area of anti-trust and securities. The reason is they need the ability to compete with the vertically integrated chains. A classic example is in Alabama where there are about 400 independent pharmacists (small business owners). The major chain pharmacies such as Walgreens, Wal-Mart, etc, have vertically integrated and combined their buying power of all their stores such that the independent pharmacies cannot compete. These 400 pharmacists banded together and created their own CoOp (horizontally integrated). They purchased first their generic drugs together, and then they expanded into a multi-billion dollar operation saving them millions yearly and making them more competitive. Had they not used a CoOp, they would have been sued for anti-trust. This is an excellent example of how the use of social entrepreneurship improved the community.

Democratic Governance. Democratic governance is better than dictators. The concept is that the members or citizens vote, either for themselves or through representatives (like the US Congress and House of Representatives today), and decide the rules by which the organization will operate in society. Unfortunately history teaches use that democracies ultimately degenerate into a *gang in possession* (often because of special interest or lobbyist groups) and finally decline into a dictatorship. Democracies often gather into Federal groupings. Federal by definition is a monarchy over a democracy as soon as the powers in charge cease to be servants and become tyrants (the gang in possession). We are seeing this all over the world as democracy after democracy falls to dictatorship, usually because the people have become entitlement hungry and their economy falls apart. Tytler said,

"Once the people (members) determine they can vote themselves largely from the public (or company) treasury the democracy (socialist governance) collapses over loose fiscal policy, always followed by a dictatorship" (emphasis added). His words, not mine!

Elements of the Collaborative Economy

Collaborative Entrepreneur. In his paper published in the Spring 2011 edition of *innovations Technology| Governance | Globalization*, Bill Drayton (who pioneered the term "social entrepreneurship" and was voted by U.S. News & World Report as one of America's Top 25 Leaders), said,

> *The world for 10,000 years has been run by a few people... The new model is already here. It is a world where everyone is a change maker, not just tiny elite... This new world will be a global team of teams, teams that come together in varying combinations, scales, and intensities as the need requires. The faster things change, the more the world will need this giant, fast-moving kaleidoscope of teams. A team is only a team when all its members are players; and in a world defined by escalating change, they can only be players if they contribute* ("Collaborative Entrepreneurship – How Social Entrepreneurs Have Learned to Tip the World by Working in Global Teams," Spring 2011 Edition, pages 1-5).

I will address this more in chapter 8 – The Framisdortin.

I believe what Bill is saying is that it will take the best of the entrepreneurs and social entrepreneurs to create the collaborative entrepreneur teams that will be needed in the 21st century. My friend, Dan Robles, heads the Ingenesist Project or what he calls the "Crowd Think Tank." Dan and I were panel members in January 2014 at the *Future of Money and Technology Summit* in San Francisco leading the discussion of Community *Crypto-Currency*. Dan has often said, "That in the future, everyone will be a corporation." (An LLC or other company form works too.) I think we three would agree that in the immediate future, the most successful projects will be operated in a collaborative structure where individual "members or players" with excellence will bring about massive change in business, the social agenda, and future governance. I call that change Collaborative Commonwealth™.

EcoSystem Centered. The Economic System (EcoSystem) is a hybrid of both finance and the environment. The collaborative entrepreneur is a business minded and a socially conscious innovator. He or she is concerned with sustainability and the environmental impact the project will have on the community and the world.

Share Mindset. If everything is free, then there is no incentive to create new ideas, and if everything is scarce, then only a limited few can prosper. The collaborative entrepreneur seeks a reasonable financial gain, provides for society's needs, and shares ideas and opportunities with an open-hand versus closed hand.

The question one has to ask, "How much is enough?" When you look at your needs and the needs of others, if you have your needs met, you must in the future consider sharing with others who will collaborate with you to bring your ideas and concepts forward, often at a faster pace. This is not some share-the-wealth, government give-a-way-for-no-work concept; it is a reward for value-contributed concept. In the future we hope to value each individual (Drop) for their tangible and intangible Time – Talent – Treasure contributed.

Circular Integration. I believe this brings the best of vertical and horizontal integration in from the extremes to the Commons. When a project is created, its purpose (the *Why?*) is what is placed at the center, not a person or a company. Next, we gather collaborative entrepreneurs around the project each contributing their time, talent, and treasure (potential, think Ocean) to see the project come to completion. The definition of a circle is that all points (individuals, think Drops) are equidistant from the center. Collaborative Commonwealth™ can provide a governance structure to enable individuals, teams, groups, etc. (Drops, Streams, and Rivers) to collaborate, profit, and provide social benefit to the world around any concept, project, marketplace, etc. in an Ocean of potential.

Commonwealth Governance. This governance which I believe will bring balance in all four sectors: Government, For-Profit,

Non-Profit, and Cooperative is called Collaborative Commonwealth™. Collaborative Commonwealth™ is not federal, it is not democratic, it is not capitalist, and it is not socialist. It is Confederate, Republic, and Collabortist. It provides for sharing of ideas, profits and social needs. Confederate (a form of collaboration), meaning a league, an inter-governmental organization that allows each person and State by its own sovereignty to remain or succeed from the league if the government "of the people and by the people" is not upheld. This is just the beginning look at how this new form of governance will produce a world changing Collaborative Economy.

(See Thought Mastery Next Page)

Thought Mastery

There is a need for change in how our nation governs. The chart that follows captures the issues.

Industrial Economy	Social Economy	Collaborative Economy
Centered on Accumulation of Wealth (Self)	Centered in Distribution of Wealth (Network)	Centered in Sharing Access to Wealth (EcoSystem or EcoSphere)
Self Centered or Scarcity Mindset	Free or Entitlement Mindset	Pro-Rata Share Mindset
Vertically Integrated	Horizontally Integrated	Circularly Integrated
Dictator Power At The Top	Democracy Small Group Control	Commonwealth Individual Power

You should understand the differences between a capitalist entrepreneur, a social entrepreneur, and a Collaboratist entrepreneur.

Chapter 5 – Collaborative Economics: Multiply not Divide

The Money Dilemma. Going back to medieval days, the form of exchange for time, goods, and services was barter. If I made shoes and you raised chickens we could exchange shoes for chickens and both our needs would be met. However, if I made shoes and you made guns and I did not need a gun or you did not need shoes we were at an impasse.

E. C. Reigel in his 1944 book entitled, *Private Enterprise Money- A Non-Political Money System,* wrote about how barter was changed with a commodity saying,

> *Their first expedient to escape simple barter was to hit upon some common commodity that would be acceptable to most any trader*

and which would not deteriorate in storage. A number of such commodities were used, but it was natural that ultimately gold and silver would be selected as the best suited for the purpose. They were the most portable, because much value was represented by small weight, and they were not subject to erosion. (page 16)

Adam Smith is considered to be the father of modern economics. In his book *An Inquiry into the Nature and Causes of the Wealth of Nations* (1776), Smith debates the functionality of barter, stating that there was a need for "a medium of exchange" independent of one's ability to produce a commonly required commodity. He was saying people need something that can be exchanged that is independent of our personal production, for example gold and silver.

Money is said to have four purposes:

1. A medium of exchange, independent of commodity or labor
2. We can use it as a store of value until we need it at a later date
3. Pay debts or otherwise meet our contractual obligations
4. A way of keeping score as a unit of accounting.

Smith's theory, steeped in his belief that the most useful purpose of money is as a medium of exchange, allows for the emergence of capitalism and even the modern day banking system which is based in credit (debt). We should note that money only affects the price of a thing (its value), not the process of physical production. Value is whatever two people agree it is – an agreement, contract, or covenant.

Alfred Mitchell Innes, author of *The Credit Theory of Money* (1914), disagrees with Smith's statements on the theory of barter and a method of exchange by introducing a concept called the exchange of a commodity for a credit that is based on an agreed upon "unit of exchange." Proposing this would solve the aforementioned impasse as the gun seller could simply accept a credit slip for the sale and use it wherever that credit would be accepted. Innes goes on to say that true barter as an exchange has never really existed. Here is his comment by reference:

> *The Credit Theory is this: that a sale and purchase is the exchange of a commodity for a credit. From this main theory springs the sub-theory that the value of credit or money does not depend on the value of any metal or metals, but on the right which the creditor acquires to 'payment,' that is to say, to satisfaction for the credit, and on the obligation of the debtor to 'pay' his debt, and conversely on the right of the debtor to release himself from his debt by the tender of an equivalent debt owed by the creditor, and the obligation of the creditor to accept this tender in satisfaction of his credit.* (The Banking Law Journal, Volume 31 by Alfred F. White (page 152)).

Credits or credit as a proven form of commerce dates back to Babylon and pre-dates coinage or what we call currency today. Currency is defined as the money in use by a country (or any order, i.e. community) and money is defined as the pieces of metal or paper or credit that enables citizens to have the faith to buy, exchange, or sell goods and services. Crypto-currency (i.e. BitCoin, points, rewards, etc.) may add the digital element to currency. (See chapter 7 – Collaborative Commonwealth in Commerce for more on this topic.)

So it follows that assets are the accumulation of currency (as well as other valuable objects that you can claim in ownership both tangible and intangible) above the basic needs, emergency, and lifestyle. So let's contrast that with capital.

In his book, *The Mystery of Capital*, Hernando De Soto states, "Capital is the force that raises the productivity of labor and creates the wealth of nations" (page 5). So it is reasonable to say that a nation without capital cannot be capitalistic. In Collaborative Economics, we cannot or should not discount the value of the (human) contribution of talent that produced the product or service. Human contribution is more than labor as an expense item; it can be argued that it is part of the value proposition (the value of the thing), otherwise why would we value art from one painter over another in an art collection?

Assets that can be invested become capital. Assets must be able to have a title (the right to claim ownership to property) to represent them. Without title, capital, according to De Soto, is "dead capital" (pages 30 – 37) and unable to be multiplied into wealth. The reason that most of the world has dead capital is there exists no system of title or the process to obtain title is so lengthy that it is called "extralegal" (page 21). He further states extralegal real estate, in third world nations, is valued in excess of $9.3 Trillion. **The Collaborative Economy must eliminate** *dead capital* **and develop a system to properly value tangible assets and intangible assets** (see chapter 7). I find it fascinating, that because of antiquated document system and poor governance, the poor control more wealth than the rich and the poor cannot do anything about it in today's economy because they cannot convert it into capital as it is understood in the Old Economy, which definitely needs to be fixed.

Capitalism is an economic system in which investments in the ownership (title) of the means of production, distribution, and exchange (buying and selling) of wealth (assets and currency) is maintained chiefly by private individuals or corporations. This is not as true for CoOps or government as a means of ownership. First consider that capitalism is private not government-based. It is profit not non-profit. Capitalism is strictly tied to title or ownership and the ability to buy or sell in which ever way individuals or corporations might agree, covenant, or contract. As we go forward this is an important fact.

Capitalism was conceived in the 19th century as a product of the Industrial Revolution (refer to chapters 3 and 4); then Socialism and Communism came about as an answer to uncontrolled capitalism (in the extremes). These *isms* are from the last cycle of power and do not accurately reflect the economic doctrines that will apply to the Collaborative Economy in the 21st century. In my research, I found one source which showed there are at least *234-*

isms (Source: phrontistery.info/isms.html) which express or state of health, doctrines, methods, as well as philosophical governmental, moral, religious and political belief systems. That is right; **capitalism is a belief system not a form of governance as some might think. It is more akin to a religion than it is governance.**

Collaborative Commonwealth™ is about governance, it is not capitalism, certainly not socialism; let's just call it collaboratism. What is the difference? Capitalism allocates profit to the individual in proportion to their ownership; Socialism allocates equal distribution, independent of ownership or contribution. It did not work with the pilgrims, it does not work in communist countries, and it will not work as a belief system in the 21st century. Those are all *social fiction* designed to keep *power in the hands of a few;* no different than a dictatorship. Collaboratism creates *power in the hands of many and distribute profits pro-rata based on the contributions by the individual.* Collaborative Commonwealth™ then governs how this distribution of power and profit takes place while respecting the individuals' rights who collaborated in the agreement or covenant.

Division – Its Broken

Money is divisible by design. The current or *old system* of world economics uses money that is created from credit also known as fiat money.

In chapters 3 and 4, we learned that there are 250 year cycles and there are also 40 and 80 year cycles. If these S curves are right, we may be headed for yet another financial crisis (collapse) before 2016. How do you think this may affect the elections? I am not sure either side understands the problem or can offer a solution; they are stuck in the old system (the legacy system, remember our discussion earlier of cell towers and their investor's ROI?). The current party system is a legacy system.

The Central Banking System (in the US we call it the Federal Reserve, which is neither federal, nor a reserve, but *a private corporation acting as a bank* [a critical element of the fix]) published a workbook entitled *Modern Money Mechanics* (May 1961 Dorthy M. Nichols) which proposes how to use debt (credits) as a lever. It describes how the fractional reserve banking system or its *fiat* currency works by division. To save time, you can read chapter 5 in *Why Divide When You Can Multiply?*, or go to YouTube.com and watch any number of videos on The Fed, How Money Works, Fiat Currency and you will get the concept. Suffice it to say the Central Banking System is a failing system, which has to change. It has been the cause of *economic slavery* around the world.

Forms of Slavery. *Economic Slavery* is when you work for your house, your food, and they pay you enough to pay for the house yourself (a byproduct of Capitalism). *Physical Slavery* is when you work or don't work and the state or your master provides you a house and food to eat (a byproduct of Socialism). We are currently moving toward Physical Slavery in the U.S. despite our so called freedom. Like Tytler said, "We vote from the treasury largely."

All these so called *entitlements* encourage the nanny-state (someone to watch over me)! Don't misunderstand me, the poor will always be with us, and society should plan for their assistance; but we should not create or encourage dependency. I believe this assistance should come from the local community, not a national government. We fought the Civil War and for our Civil Rights in America, at a great cost of life and property; surely we will not give that over to a corporation (the *Fed* bank) or a governmental master (dictator) so easily for a few measly so-called benefits which we pay for anyway in reality.

I think President Lincoln may have said it best:

> *The 'money powers' prey on the nation in times of peace and adversity. The banking powers are more despotic than monarchy, more insolent than autocracy, more selfish than bureaucracy. They denounce as public enemies all who question their methods or throw light upon their crimes. I have two great enemies, the Southern Army in the front of me, and the bankers in the rear. Of the two, the one at my rear is my greatest foe. The 'money power' will endeavor to prolong its reign by working upon the prejudices of the people until the wealth is aggregated in the hands of a few and the Republic is destroyed.* (Presidential quote: August 1861 after first income tax was passed.)

Well said, Mr. President. Was this the reason he was assonated?

I find it quite interesting that in 1913 when the Central Bank was created, the government also enacted the Income Tax Law that would allow the government to take from our labor the money to pay for this credit-based system (fiat capital). The world economy is controlled by Central Banks. It is already interconnected, such that the failure on one could cause the domino effect of the failure of many, if not all of them. Without a parallel system where *reformation* can take place, we may not have learned how to spell CRISIS yet!

Multiplication – The Fix

If the current old economic system used by the world is based in division, then the fix is likely 180 degrees in the opposite direction. The opposite of division is multiplication.

Multiplication not Percentage Increase. When we earn currency from our labor, we pay our bills and if we do not have *too much month and the end of our money;* then we have what is called *discretionary income* or *personal capital.* We have two choices: 1) we can spend it, or 2) we can save it. In America today, most people choose to spend it. According to StatisticBrain.com, which compiled their statistics from Federal Reserve, U.S. Census Bureau, and the IRS; the average American family has, as of July 2012, the following (averages):

- Household income - $43,000
- Home Value - $160,000

- Home Mortgage - $95,000
- Household Debt - $117,951
- Savings for Retirement - $35,000
- Savings for Emergency - $3,800
- Credit Card Debt - $2,200
- 1:4 say they will have to postpone retirement
- 1:5 believe they will have enough money to retire
- 1:2 are not even saving for retirement
- 1:3 has money for an emergency

How do you compare to the averages? While in 2008 the cost of living is increasing, household incomes are decreasing, and bankruptcies are on the rise. If we don't reform we will become economic slaves! I don't think it has gotten any better in 2014.

Simple Compounded Interest. Interest is a fraction (division), 1% interest is 1/100 or .01. If you take your savings times "1" plus your interest rate, you get your annual savings. If you leave it to accumulate, it compounds. $1,000 X 1.01 = $1,010 and year 2... $1,010 X 1.01 = $1,020.10. The .10 is the compounding. This IS NOT how to multiply your time, talent, or treasure; this is a path to economic slavery!

The Rule of 72's is a banking rule that says if you take 72 and divide it by your current interest rate on savings, it approximates how long it takes your money to double. Consider that 72/1% (the current saving rate) that is 72 years! If inflation is at 4% (and it is currently much higher) the cost of living double every 18 years (72/4 = 18). We are not going to make it if we don't reform. A system of division (based on percentage yield) never makes you FREE, it only creates economic slaves!

I think by now you get it, the current economic system is designed to create economic slaves. Your God-given individual rights are to be FREE, not be a slave. So let's consider what multiplication can do for us.

Owning Not Renting Your Life. In my books, *Solving The Puzzle of Owning A Franchise—Stop Renting Your Life And Start Owning It Instead* and in *Wealth 3.0 – Saving America One Small Business At A Time;* I talk about owning your life and not renting it to someone else for a fraction of what you are worth.

A typical business spends about 25% on labor and 50% on operations and 25% goes to the owner. So in this scenario (25 – 50 – 25), if you were the labor and the owner you would have 50% of the profits, not your share of the 25% with the labor force. Said another way, "If you want to multiply your income – fire your boss and then go into business for yourself!" The thought of this makes about 90% of American's tremble.

However, before you quit your job, you have to figure cost of goods (COG) into this equation. The scenario above of 25 – 50 – 25 has to be multiplied by the gross margin (GM). GM = Total Income – COG; so the more a product costs at wholesale the lower the profit. For example, if a hamburger sells for $9.00 at your favorite sports bar, the food cost is about $3.00 and the GM is about $6.00. If you are a professional consultant trading your time for money your COG is likely $0. If you are a manufacturer that has to sell through a distribution channel then your GM might be as low as 10%.

This simple analysis will allow you to pick the right business if you decide to fire your boss. $(25 - 50 - 25) \times$ GM will help you determine your budget and evaluate your business. Let's use the hamburger one more time. If you sell $100,000 worth of hamburgers, your COG is about $33,000 and your GM is about $67,000. It will cost you about $34,000 to run the operation and you and the employees will have to live on $33,000. Clearly, if you can only generate $100,000 in sales you should not be in the hamburger business.

Bottom line, owning a business is like having a job, they both have risk involved. If the owner does not watch the costs of doing business (the 50%) or fails to get enough top line income (sales), the business may fail. Truth is that in the first 10 years, the way the system is today, about 90% of businesses fail due to lack of capital or lack of a good business plan.

The question is do you want to leave this risk management to someone else? If so, then you should be an employee. **If you want to protect your freedom and multiply your income, you should be your own boss.** It really is just that simple. We will look more at this later as we look at many other scenarios of the Collaborative Economy and how we might be able to reduce risk.

Ask yourself the question, *Do I own title to my labor (freedom) or does someone else own title to my labor (economic slavery)?*

Investing Instead Of Working. I am sure you have heard that "the rich get richer and the poor get poorer." It is true! The rich have economic freedom and the poor are economic slaves. Considering the average family statistics cited earlier in this chapter, the average family has very little or nothing to invest. Remember money you can invest converts your assets into capital.

The first rule of investing is Capital Preservation. If it is hard to save, you don't want to lose it. The Investment Pyramid (depicted below) is low risk at the bottom and high risk at the top. Consider:

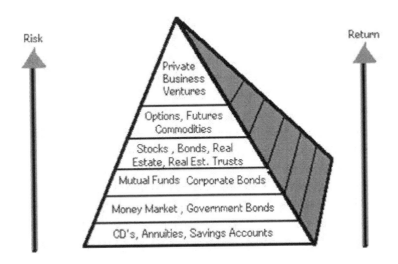

If owning a business is high risk, then why would I recommend you consider owning your own life? It is only risky if you don't know what you are doing. If you do your due diligence and seek sound advice and don't do stupid things, owning a business can be very rewarding. Your boss or the owner of the company where you work has figured it out and hired you! Aren't you as smart as he/she is? Or have you become satisfied in your economic slavery?

The trouble is that most do not have a plan, nor do they have the right finances when they start. A wise friend once told me, "A good plan executed poorly almost always works; but a poor plan executed to perfection almost always fails." The secret is what will multiply and get you to your goals? How is your current plan working? Do you have a plan? Are you an economic slave? If not, get an advisor, a budget, and a plan and overcome!

Most advisors and experts tell you to:

- have a plan
- work your plan
- pay your bills first
- save for an emergency
- and then invest from your excess.

In this book, I am discussing concepts to help you multiply. **However, I cannot render legal, accounting, or financial advice. You are encouraged to find a licensed professional to become your coach or advisor and help you in this matter.**

Thought Mastery

De Soto…"Capital is a force that raises productivity of labor and creates the wealth of nations"… Assets must have title to become capital, if not, they are "dead capital" and unable to be multiplied into wealth and are called "extralegal."

The Collaborative Economy must develop a system to properly value tangible and intangible assets.

Currency which is based in debt (fiat) is dying and will not be sustainable.

Economic or Fiscal Slavery is when you work for your house, your food, and they pay you just enough to pay for all that.

Physical Slavery is when someone else pays for your house, etc. It is a form of entitlement.

Wealth does not come from percentage increase, but from multiplication. Do you understand the Rule of 72 and how to apply it in your life? Are you committed to "own your life" or "to rent your life out" for someone else to multiply their wealth using your talent? Write in your journal how you feel about this right now.

This book cannot render legal, accounting, or financial advice. You are encouraged to find a licensed professional to become your coach or advisor and help you with your finances.

CHAPTER 6 – PRINCIPLES OF COLLABORATIVE COMMONWEALTH™

The Story of the Teacher and the Student

There once was a student who decided to pursue his calling by seeking knowledge, understanding, and wisdom so that he could emerge as a leader and fulfill his purpose. He asked his grandfather for wisdom. His grandfather said, "Find a collaborator, not a competitor. It is my experience that you need to find someone who has already done what you want to do and let them 'teach you' how to do it. Don't find a competitor who will likely send you off in a direction that allows them to have an advantage over you." *Wow*, the student thought, *my grandfather is wise; I will go find a collaborative teacher.*

After searching, the student found a good collaborative teacher. The teacher said, "To succeed you must learn the Four Principles of Multiplication." The student said, "Tell me more; I want to learn how to multiply and prosper in this Collaborative Economy!" The teacher agreed and began to share **The Four Principles of Multiplication to Prosper in the Collaborative Economy**:

Principle 1: The Principle of the Harvest. Citing an old text, the teacher shared the first principle, "Since the beginning of time, man has studied his environment. He observed that animals and plants alike replicate after their own kind. Therefore, whatever you do, make sure that it can be duplicated. There can be no multiplication if it can't be duplicated."

The teacher continued, "From a single seed of corn, you can grow a corn plant. That plant will produce 6 to 10 ears of corn. Each ear of corn has literally hundreds of seeds. If you manage your seed wisely you can eat and also multiply your harvest. Eventually, if you work your plan well, from a **single seed you can feed a nation**." (Remember in chapter 1 we talked about the Robertson Ocean. From a single idea (seed)—a duck call—several new marketplaces were created and massive wealth generated through one good idea that prospered.)

The teacher further explained this principle, "You must:

a) **Sow with a purpose and not in chaos.** You cannot be careless with your seed. Protect it; make sure you sow it into fertile ground, not hard soil where there is no hope of growing. Remember that **every seed has the potential to feed a nation.**

b) **Don't scatter your seed greater than you can plow.** You cannot grow too fast, especially where you don't control your environment. **You are the steward of your harvest.**

c) **Always plant more than you need.** The first thing you must do is decide – **How much is enough?** Once you have enough for yourself and enough seed to plant for the future, you must generate excess for Principle 4. **Don't be greedy with your prosperity; treat it with an open hand and be willing to share."**

Adding further clarity to this principle, the teacher said, "You always reap in a different season than you sow. Timing is an important part of planting. If you plant in the wrong season, you won't reap good results. If you use all your resources to plant, you will have none when it is time to harvest. Therefore plan carefully and manage your seed, time, and harvest by ensuring you have the resources to accomplish all three."

The teacher said, "Let's move on, to **Principle 2: If You Don't Take a Risk, You Won't Multiply.**" The student, looking puzzled, asked "But, I have been told all my life not to take a risk."

The teacher smiled and cited another very old text, "There was a business man who needed to go on a trip, and so he brought in his three managers and gave them each an assignment. To the first, he gave a project with 10 elements, the next 5 elements, and to the other a project with 2 elements."

The business man said, "Each of you use your best efforts to grow these projects in my absence." Upon returning after a long period of time, the business owner called in each project manager one by one and inquired of their status. The first project manager said, "Sir, I have been very productive I have expanded your project from 10 to 20 elements and we are very profitable."

The business owner called in the second project manger to give his report, "Sir, I have expanded your project from 5 to 10 elements and we are very profitable."

Then the third project manager was called to give his report, "Well sir, I know you are a conservative man, very successful and if I had taken a risk with your project, you might have lost it. So, I maintained your project and it is safe."

The business owner, rocked back in his chair and said, "Project Manager 1, you have multiplied my wealth, you have been faithful in small things, I will make you a Vice President over an entire division. Project Manager 2, you too have been faithful, you will get a pay raise. Project Manager 3, I left you in charge of my assets, you did not take a risk, you did not multiply, you sought only to preserve. As a result we have fallen behind, and your project is now canceled. You are fired!"

Stunned, the student asked the teacher, "Why were the two who took the risks rewarded and the one who protected the owner's property was fired?"

The teacher explained, "Without the willingness to take a risk, there can be no multiplication of wealth. By playing it safe, your business falls into the hands of inflation, competitors, and the future can be lost. For this reason the manager was fired." (Remember, our earlier discussions of compound interest, the Rule of 72, and owning not renting your life.)

The student asked, "What is the next principle?" **Principle 3: The Principle of Excess – Investing with Others Capital.** The teacher began with another story from the ancient text that teaches about a miracle.

Five thousand people had gathered to hear a prophet speak. They were hungry so the prophet asked his helpers to find someone with excess food. There was a young boy who had loaves and fishes, more than he needed but not enough to feed all 5,000. The prophet said, 'Bring me the food.' He gave thanks, prayed and began to break the bread and fishes into pieces. Amazingly, he multiplied the food and fed everyone. Upon picking up the food that remained, the helpers discovered there were 12 baskets full, which they able to return to the boy and others.

The teacher went on to say, "The lesson here is that when you take from an investor and you multiply it for good, you must repay the investor's principal with a good profit."

The student replied, "I get that, but why did they give to the boy and others." The teacher said, "We will discover that in **Principle 4: The Principle of Gleaning, Sharing or Caring for Others.**"

The teacher continued the lesson, "In this 4th Principle, there was a certain farmer who planted a crop. As the crop matured and was ready to harvest, the farmer came and harvested his crop and made an excellent profit. However, there were others less fortunate in the village than he, so he left the corners and the edges so the poor could also have something to eat."

The teacher further explained, "Once you know **how much is enough**, if you can leave the excess for the less fortunate without fear of loss, it will bless them and you." Giving thanks to his teacher, the student went away to a quiet place to record what he had learned in his journal. (You might do the same now too.) Remember, the Robertson's (Duck Dynasty) give thanks also, they have learned these principles.

Agile not Fragile

The Collaborative Economy is not the same as the Old Economy. History teaches us that our economy models our technology in warfare. Interestingly, war has often been used as a cure for a bad economy.   (Reading E. C. Riegel's book mentioned in chapter 5 will document how close war and money really are.)

In the beginning, warfare was large in scale and yet very *fragile*. We would stand across a field of fire and we would shoot arrows, throw spears, or fire guns until the last man stood or the other side retreated. Once that happened, we took possession of the land. Later, as the military industrialized into complex, fantastic machines of war (tanks, airplanes, and battleships) we widened our reach, and we lobbed even larger weapons at each other, ultimately atomic in nature, until our enemy surrendered.

By the Vietnam War, tactics changed. The Vietnamese, using guerrilla warfare, were *agile* and despite our war machines, their *agile* tactics caused great casualties and confusion. They didn't follow the old rules, they *reformed* warfare.

As technology improves, so does our agility. Today the majority of military actions are by *Special Forces*. SEALS have evolved to where five to six men in a rubber boat can call fire down from above using un-piloted drones and defeat an opposition force. Special Forces are very *agile*. We can do much more with much less human risk by taking advantage of technology.

In the first real cycle of American business we were an agricultural society. The introduction of the Industrial Revolution brought machines to the farm as trains and automobiles replaced horses and buggies. Technology, mass transit and fast transit have reformed business practices too.

However, business remained extremely fragile throughout the 20th century. In 2008, we started to see the ridged fragile hierarchical business structures called "too big to fail" crumble under massive debt and fiat capital schemes. Trillions of dollars in value were lost almost overnight. The fragile Old Economy was declining and a new Agile Collaborative Economy was emerging.

The lesson-learned: if we are to survive, we have to build fluid agile business structures based in a collaborative structure (i.e. The Concept of Water) not the fixed fragile hierarchical structures (one-up/one-down) we find in business and government today.

Being agile not fragile is the key principle and lesson to learn.

Individual not Separate

In this principle, we need to appreciate self-value and eliminate self-centeredness. As you recall, in this form of governance we want the individual rights to be maintained and the personal and intellectual, intangible assets to be valued so that we can issue title and create capital to be invested. Remember the ideal expressed by Abraham Lincoln that the central bankers and hierarchical business leaders who seek to keep assets restrained in the *hands of a few* are our greatest enemy.

The time for self-centered leadership is over; we need to value individuals who work with each other in teams on projects in a new form of collaboration. The *lone wolf syndrome* has failed; *it takes team work to make a dream work!*

Open Hand not Closed Hand Stewards

In addition to writing books, I have an active advisory and consulting practice to for-profit businesses. I also work with non-profits and CoOps teaching collaborative principles. My wife, Cheryl-Ann, and I currently oversee the Global Stewards Initiative (GSI) and an initiative within called Stewards Summit™. *Steward* means manager or overseer. At this Summit, one of the central concepts is that we don't really own anything; it all belongs to God and we are His Stewards.

A closed-handed (a fist) person, manager, or steward is one who is looking at the lessons taught to the student earlier in this chapter, and he would say, "It is my business, I can earn a good profit, I will pay my investors back, and I will choose to give or not give from my excess to others who are in need." I think you would agree this could be a self-centered person. They are not evil; rather, they believe they are the center of their universe and it is their success. They likely don't subscribe to Leadership Emergence Theory (LET) from chapter 2. They do not believe there is an unseen hand at work, just their own efforts. They are an *"I"* person, not a *"We"* or *"Team"* person. They typically don't share.

By contrast, an open-handed person, manager, or steward is one who believes that he/she owns nothing, and when looking at the lessons taught in chapter 4, he would say, "It is God's business, God will provide enough to meet my needs, the investors must be paid back with a excellent return on investment, and the excess of the business must go to help others." I think you will agree that the open-handed person's approach is *Others Centered*, collaborates, and manages what has been given to him/her. Definitely the open-handed person is a *We* or *Team* person. They are committed to share! **Be honest, which are you?**

Collaborate not Compete

As I stated before, this is not Collaborative Socialism where we take from the rich and give to the poor or Collaborative Capitalism where we keep all the profits for a few. Each person is rewarded pro-rata according to the value of time, talent, and treasure exchanged or invested in a project. Individuals serve to fulfill their purpose, not work a job for a paycheck. It is not a dog-eat-dog, competitive environment where power is the means of success; it is a recognition based environment where the goal is TEAM over Me.

Thought Mastery

There are four principles from the story of the teacher and the student that we need to learn to Multiply and Prosper in the Collaborative Economy, and they are:

- Principle 1: The Principle of the Harvest

- o Sow with a Purpose, not into Chaos.
- o Don't scatter your seed greater than you can plow.
- o Always plant more than you need.
- o From one seed, you can feed a nation.

- Principle 2: If You Don't Take A Risk, You Won't Multiply.

- Principle 3: The Principle of Excess – Investing with Others' Capital.

- Principle 4: The Principle of Gleaning, Sharing or Caring for Others

Principles of Collaborative Commonwealth™ I should adopt in my life are:

1. I should maintain my individual rights and values, but not become an island separate from others.
2. I should strive to collaborate with others to the pro-rata (sharing) benefit of others according to their contributions to the project.
3. As an open-handed individual, manager, or steward, I should apply The Four Principles of Multiplication to Prosper in the Collaborative Economy in my life. I can be valued (sow my seed well) by multiplying my resources to meet the needs of the collaborative group and myself. If I take investors' money, I make sure they get their money back and earn an excellent return on investment. Lastly, I must determined **how much is enough** and give generously to others in need so that I can bless them and thereby be blessed. Other-centered, not self-centered is my principle.

4. I find ways to collaborate with others and seek not to labor solely for my personal gain.
5. It takes TEAM work to make a dream work, not more of me. There is rest when I collaborate with others.

Chapter 7 – Government, Society, Commerce, and Business

Collaborative Commonwealth™ - Government

In the last 100 years, the US Government as well as many other world governments has come under attack. In particular the two extremes are:

1. The capitalistic democratic countries
2. And the socialistic republics and dictatorships

In this chapter we will look at how Collaborative Commonwealth™, a new approach, will impact government, society, commerce, and business.

Democratic countries, as we discussed earlier, have taken the approach that a smaller representation group, often elected by some form of voting scheme, should develop the rules for society. When a small group like a Senate, a House of Representatives, a sub-committee, lobbyists, special interests groups, etc. seek to impose their will for their personal or corporate gain and not make decisions for the good the citizen; then, we have a *dictatorship by committee* who also often have a socialist agenda. The only real difference is that with a dictator the small control group is reduced to one person.

As I presented in Chapter 4 – Evolution to Change, the capitalist and socialist agendas, as economic systems, are failing globally. The capitalist (often a democracy/scarcity model) and the socialist (typically a dictator/free (entitlement) model) are opening the way for a third economic system called the *Collabortist* (typically a commonwealth/pro-rata sharing model).

For clarity, when I say pro-rata sharing, I refer to each individual's contribution of time, talent, and treasure, whether tangible or intangible to the project that is valued such that when the profits are distributed, each receives his or her proportionate pro-rata share.

The Need For A Reformation

Since the Christian Reformation Movement (1500's) and for 300 of the last 500 years since, when governments are called to reform, it almost always emerges as a republic form of government. (Not republican, but republic.) "Power cycles from the few back into the hands of the many." Monarchies, democracies, and advantaged control groups (kings and dictators) are toppled and individual rights are restored.

This of course was easier when there was a different place to move to (like the *New World*) because these *ideals* (not ideas) had room to flourish. In the 21st century, there is not much new land to discover. The new land may be a *virtual land* as in social media and gaming engagement via technology. Social media serves two purposes: 1) it gives individuals (Drops) a voice, and 2) like-thinking friends can fellowship and advocate their common interests, concerns, or beliefs (Streams).

Reformation in government, or an economic system, if not corrupted by small group agendas, is healthy. However, one of the by-products is often division from the status quo. Unity for a season may be broken. I contend if there was unity before, it had been *a manufactured pseudo-unity* and it will take breaking up the accepted system for the power of self-interest to be reformed and for the principles of Collaboration to be established. (see chapter 5).

Most government is top-down control, is hierarchical in structure, and uses pseudo-social agendas to cause the poor and the middle class to vote for the candidate that will provide the most entitlements (see Tytler and Marx's quote, chapter 3); while increasing government revenue through higher taxation.

By contrast a reformed government, after a struggle, returns to unity and emerges as a Republic (also called a Commonwealth) based in individual freedom and rights, and promotes a pro-rata shared mutual economic growth over governmental taxation. It also promotes a sense of self-reliance versus government-reliance and therefore reduces the burden on government to provide benefits and entitlements; therefore, the government doesn't need spend or tax as once thought. It is commonly accepted that government is not as efficient as private enterprise. (Remember chapter 6, the four principles and specifically Principle 4, Gleaning).

What We Learned In the "Occupy Movement"

In 2011, New Your City and hundreds of other cities around the world saw the convergence of social media and reformation. The uncorrupted focus of the *Occupy Movement* was against social and economic inequality. It sought to stop vertical governance and move toward distributed collaborative governance. It began without a declared agenda, it was leadership emerging with a conscious thought, *the system doesn't work, let's fix it.*

Emphasis was placed on how big corporations, like big government has used its influence to constrain wealth and access to capital to a limited few. The slogan *We are the 99%* said it all, that the one percent (1%) had to give back. The purest of Occupy advocates were not socialist or communist; they were concerned citizens of an emerging Collaborative Movement.

They sought what this book is trying to awaken in you; that Collaborative Commonwealth™ is the answer; but big government and big business sought to discredit this movement and called them either Socialist or Communist. After several months of tolerance, their opposition launched all matter of white and black propaganda into television and the other forms of media to discredit this movement, saying, "It might move from reformation to revolution." Governments, out of fear of loss, called it terrorism to discredit the Occupy Movement. When this country was formed it was called patriotism, now it is terrorism since it was contrary to the (dictator's) purpose. I was not an Occupy person; but I appreciated their efforts to bring reform to our broken government and business systems.

If you recall in the Introduction, I spoke about the "fear of loss being greater than the desire for gain." Here big business and big government feared a change in the status quo that kept them on top. **The mistake the Occupy Movement made was to not have established leadership and vision from the beginning to guard the ideals of the movement.** This allowed propaganda to creep in.

Remember, what caused the movement to grow was the lack of a clear agenda! (Open and Free). As outside influence crept in, similar to a computer virus, new agendas emerged many good and some bad and the movement stalled *in committee.* The 99% felt equal sharing of ideals was the way. This was a critical mistake as it was deemed socialist. Pro-rata sharing was the correct choice. Leadership emergence is critical in the early stages of a movement (see chapter 2) committees don't work. Like water, we need to be agile and flow around these obstacles as the Collaborative Movement expands.

As a reformation in government emerges, Drops, Steams, and Rivers will have to emerge. Unity in the new governance should follow Collaborative Commonwealth™ principles allowing freedom with responsibility from the bottom up with pro-rata sharing of the profits according to one's investment (contribution value) of time, talent, and treasure.

Is Our Government Broken?

In short, YES! That said, I choose the United States as my home sweet home. We can effect change; but we don't need to overthrow our government, just reform it. It will be a bottom-up movement, not a top down. Young people will lead the way, they are better connected. They collaborate more than compete. The age 55+ crowd will need to invest in their youth. New projects, systems, structures, and networks will need to emerge. We will have to move from a scarcity mindset (competition) to a collaborative mindset (pro-rata sharing).

We must break the entitlement mindset (free) in the process. You can't spend more than you earn; and you can't borrow yourself out of debt; but you can collaborate to overcome.

Why Collaborative Commonwealth™
As Opposed To A Republic Or A Democracy?

As I began to revisit American history I found myself confused at first. What should be clear, but was not, is how we as a nation should govern.

I have never had ambition for politics, I am a businessman, I am a husband, I am a father, and I am a grandfather. I care about people. Therefore, as I write down these thoughts, I do so to hopefully bring clarity as to why I believe we need a *reformation* of the current approach to how we execute governance in this country. It made sense for Martin Luther and it made since for Martin Luther King, Jr. I am not an anarchist. I believe we need governance (order), I believe our founding fathers were inspired by the Creator, and I believe that for the most part they had it right; however, society does change with time and innovation and America needs to meet the needs of *we the people!*

I believe in the principles of our Republic and I agree we need a Constitution as a form of governance that protects people from the frailties or our leadership. The Tenth Amendment says it best, "The powers not delegated to the United States by the Constitution, nor prohibited by it to the States, are reserved to the States respectively, or to the people"(emphasis added). Today the union is failing under its concept of federal governance, we are not *indivisible* we are in fact divided! We need a reformation, a change to a form more aligned with our Constitution. I believe that this is confederate (a form of collaboration), meaning a league, an inter-governmental organization that allows each person and State by its own sovereignty to remain or succeed if the government "of the people and by the people" is not upheld. This provides transparency and accountability. It also leaves the power at the lowest level widely distributed such that tyranny and dictatorship are almost impossible. I believe it was the intent of our founders to escape tyranny, monarchs, and dictators.

The Bill of Rights, the first 10 amendments to our Constitution, speaks of many things. Our First Amendment provides for no state religion, but establishes each citizen's right and freedom to have religion, free speech, a free press, allow people to assemble, and to petition the government with our grievances. Has this been lost? In this reformation I claim our First Amendment rights!

I believe in the defense of our nation, and demand our Second and Third Amendment rights to provide for that defense and for each citizen to freely choose to own a firearm or weapon be upheld.

I believe the Fourth Amendment protects our privacy and the sovereignty of our homes and the government cannot invade them by any means without a proper warrant. We are innocent until proven guilty; don't treat our citizens as terrorists!

I believe in the Fifth through the Eight Amendments. There needs to be a judicial system to enforce the rule of law codified by the people and that this should be given to each state and only in the event of conflict between states should the government intervene to promote the common peace and societal good.

I believe in the Ninth and Tenth Amendment as to personal rights and our rights are vested in the people.

We live in difficult times. Business and government has forgotten its mandate for freedom and has become more dictatorial. The Thirteenth Amendment prohibits slavery. In Collaborative

Commonwealth™ I believe we should do away with all slavery, economic and physical! We need a robust economic environment where small business can thrive and individuals have the freedom to choose their livelihood without excessive governmental regulation. We need to fight against sex trade slavery!

Basically, I agree with the 27 amendments, so why propose a governmental change to a Collaborative Commonwealth™? I believe that the average American does not know the difference between a Republic and Democracy. That our government, acting as a Democracy, has become a "gang in possession," unchecked by power, and the intent of our founders has been lost! During the reformation leading to Collaborative Commonwealth™, the Republic will be restored, rights will be restored to the people, power will be decentralized, states will be responsible for their own citizen's care and needs, and taxes will be redistributed for maximum effectiveness. This is freedom with responsibility.

This reformed government will still have the Executive, Legislative, and Judicial Branches. The Executive will oversee the will of the people as a "servant leader." The Legislative will provide a voice for the will of the people, and the Judicial shall provide resolution to disputes of the people over the rule of law. I think there should be two-term limits set for each branch as with the president. The national government will provide for a common defense of the homeland and defend against all foreign enemies, but it should not be a global hegemon superpower, policing the world. It should resolve conflicts of law between the states in interstate commerce and transportation. It should collaborate with the states in Education, Health, Welfare, and Environmental issues by providing standards based on best practices. As for finance, the taxes shall be voted by the people, such to provide a balanced budget. I think we need a flat tax shared with the states and administered by the states sales tax process, which already exists. Lastly, the reformed nation should move toward debt freedom, its currency should be realigned with both tangible and intangible assets, thus increasing property rights, with the elimination of fiat capital. A true community currency exchange should be created to support intrastate, interstate, and global commerce. The central banking system should be eliminated as it is known today and banks regulated by the states.

This cannot happen overnight. Likely, it will take 20 or more years. It is like weight loss, a person didn't become overweight in one day, and it won't come off in one day either; weight loss is a process of eating less and moving more. Well, in our country becoming debt free is **a process of spending less and earning more!**

Collaborative Commonwealth™ - Society

As we ended the first decade of the 21st century, social media has become a means by which individuals network and collaborate on a wide variety of topics. For example, LinkedIn is a social network of professionals. LinkedIn officially launched on May 5, 2003. At the end of the first month in operation, LinkedIn had a total of 4,500 members in the network. As of September 30, 2011 (the end of the third quarter), professionals are signing up to join LinkedIn at a rate that is faster than two new members per second. As of November 3, 2011, LinkedIn operates the world's largest professional network on the Internet with more than 135 million members in over 200 countries and territories. In 8.5 years, from 4,500 to over 135 million. This is called viral growth.

Facebook from a dorm room in February 2004, they reached one million users by that yearend, and as of March 2013 they reported in excess of one billion total users. This is almost three times the U.S. population.

At the end of 2010, according to InSites Consulting, 72% of the entire Internet user population worldwide is a member of at least one social network. According to *Internet World* statistics there are over two billion Internet users, therefore if social media networking were a nation, its 72% membership would weigh in around 1.5 billion people, which is larger than China whose 1.3 billion people form the most populous nation on earth. Facebook alone has almost achieved this status.

> **Any future aspect of global planning must consider:**
> **1) social networks/circles,**
> **2) electronic commerce, and**
> **3) the multicultural aspects of this collaboration.**

The financial impact should this group unite as a consumer organization, would control not only the majority of goods and services, but could declare its own private community currency.

During third quarter 2014, we intend to launch a social network (a movement) called CollaborateUSA.com. If you are committed to this concept of reformation, then go to this website and join the movement!

Social Contract Theory. Since the time of Plato, philosophers and governmental thought leaders have wrestled with *Social Contract Theory*. Today we hear words like *social justice* or the Occupy Movement we discussed earlier in this chapter. These are various views, ranging across all governance concepts; many of the ideals were formed in the 17th century on how people organize themselves into a society (capitalism or socialism).

Philosophers such as Hugo Grotius, Thomas Hobbes, John Locke, Jean-Jacques Rousseau and Pierre-Joseph Proudhon are among many noted writers on Social Contract Theory.

Equalitarianism as a doctrine meaning *equal* is a trend of thought that favors equality and contains the idea of equity and quality. This means that people should be treated the same regardless of societal diversity of race, religion, ethnicity, sex, sexual orientation, politics, socioeconomic status, ability or disability and heritage. Further, in economics, Equalitarianism is a state in which equality of outcome has been structured for all the participants. Cooperatives certainly follow this concept to ensure better market price for all the producers. I agree that we are equal as to rights, but each person should earn pro-rata from our value exchange to a project or business.

When we look at society today, it is not equal at all. Thomas Hobbs, in his book *Leviathan* (circa 1660), argues that society (the Commonwealth) needs to be ruled by a sovereign (in one of three forms: 1) monarchy, 2) democracy and 3) aristocracy). Benjamin Franklin, in 1787, said, "In free governments, the rulers are the servants and the people are their superiors or sovereigns." Rousseau and Hobbs, believed that individual representation was "indivisible" and inalienable" and one's individual religious beliefs were the sovereign. I believe individual sovereignty (the Drop) is the key to reformation. (*Democracy*, page 5, edited by Ellen Frankel Paul, Fred Dycus Miller, and Jeffery Paul).

These concepts converged in the mind of Thomas Jefferson and others in drafting The Declaration of Independence. These patriots believed that any social contract that would compromise one's inalienable rights would de facto be voided and non-binding on any citizen. I believe this is why they condensed all these concepts into "We hold these truths to be self-evident, that all men are created equal, that they are endowed by their Creator with certain unalienable rights to life, liberty and the pursuit of happiness." If you notice, I used inalienable and unalienable as both are used in the founder's documents. They mean the same thing. See http://www.ushistory.org/declaration/unalienable.htm

What is confusing about the following words: truths, self-evident, all men, created equal, endowed by their Creator, unalienable rights, life, liberty, and pursuit of happiness? Why have we brokered these rights away for a false sense of security in *someone to watch over us?* It is because we don't stand for anything, except for our selfish needs and desires. Society has become divided and closed handed. Fists cause fights.

By the mid 1800's, Pierre-Joseph Proudhon wrote about "individual sovereignty" as the appropriate social contract. Simply, individuals, by themselves, can refrain from coercion and governing each other by making social contract man-to-man or as we call it today peer-to-peer.

We can translate this format to a business environment, where governance is important. There is commerce and exchange between producers and consumers, and while they relate through commerce, they do not attempt to govern each other. Instead, they operate by contract (covenant or agreement) where all parties reach *mutual assent* on how the project will be achieved and how each will be compensated according to their pro-rata value exchange.

Today, the hierarchal structure (pyramid, one-up/one-down) of organizations provides a top down structure that promotes a closed pathway to success as opposed to a collaborative open-handed, bottom-up, independence (circular and equal) offered in the mutual but pro-rata sharing that takes place in Collaborative

Commonwealth™. The old ways are pervasive in society today and only recently have these new ways begun to emerge, mostly through software and social media. The Cooperative Movement has been a leader for this new form of change with the new generation of cooperatives like the Minnesota 308B cooperative association. We have a number of businesses and non-profits now employing Collaborative Commonwealth™ governance and sharing with employees and alliances.

Privacy. One of my favorite shows on television is Person of Interest. In this show, Finch is a brilliant computer programmer that developed a system to detect evil and terrorists. It uses every method, especially video surveillance, to track suspicious activity. Finch discovers that in addition to detecting evil, the system can predict when a person's life is in danger and human interaction can prevent a bad outcome. Isn't it funny that good and evil are all in one system? It has always been that way. Systems are run by people who are good and evil so our systems just mimic their operators.

According to Dictionary.com *Privacy* is defined as "To separate, seclude, and deprive others of something selectively." The concept of personal privacy means more in America than the rest of the world and some languages don't even have a word for it. This is not to be confused with inalienable and indivisible rights which are God given.

Is privacy an old idea in the 21st century? With all the sensors, cameras, social media, etc., is it an idea whose time has expired?

In reality, did it even exist? Privacy is an idea of the 20th century and is akin to scarcity, a derivative of capitalistic thinking. Open-source is the future, whether we like it or not. I am not saying that all your personal information needs to be readily available in order for economic sharing to take place or that we should give up our so called right to privacy as part of our new future. But think about it, personal privacy doesn't exist with our government; they can access anything about you. Are you protected as you think? We have to decide which battles to fight and when.

Financial privacy to avoid fraud, theft, and even identity theft we all would agree is important. The concept of Internet privacy is good, as we believe we can protect ourselves, however, it also promotes lack of transparency. **Weighing privacy against transparency will become a decision we all have to make in the 21st century in order to interact with an open and sharing system.**

Relationship and Trust. In America we hardly know our neighbors anymore. In a sales training a couple of years ago, I asked my class to do what is called a *memory jogger.* It asked relational questions like who lives to the left, right, across the street, and behind you. More than 80% of the class could not answer this question. We are divided almost everyway possible socially. We divide on religion, we divide on politics, we divide sports, and we divide in marriage as more than 50% of marriages end in divorce.

Trust is often broken because people don't say what they mean nor do they mean what they say these days. Trust is essential to a healthy relationship. Trust is essential in sharing. Do you have trust issues? How are your relationships? Today, relationships at a distance, such as Facebook® have united friends and foes alike. According to Facebook, Inc. as of March 2013 they had over 1.1 billion users. According to the World Bank, the global population was 7 billion in 2011. So basically, one in seven (1:7) people are using Facebook® today. Is it trusted? Does it provide privacy? It certainly is open; it certainly is sharing. Does it create unity? These are some of the rising social considerations as we look at how to operate a global economy and govern ourselves in the 21st century.

Social Engagement. *Engagement* is commitment to something or someone, as to wed. In society, *engagement* refers to one's participation in a community or society or to one's participation in a group. Collaboration requires engagement. Key characteristics include: 1) activity or doing something; 2) interaction or being involved; 3) a social exchange by giving and receiving from another or a group; and 4) voluntary contribution without compulsion.

Engagement is measured by participation in an activity such as how many times I go to church or a group in a month, or as with the Internet how many times I visit a website and how long do I stay. If a person intensely engages in good activity, the result is health and happiness. If a person intensely engages in bad activity, the result is poor health and loss of happiness. Being engaged in too much brings on stress. The point here is balance and discernment. If you choose collaboration, you need to know who you are collaborating with and how to balance your social engagement to protect your health and happiness.

Collaborative Commonwealth™ - Commerce

Suppose you awoke this morning and like the TV show *Revolution* you discovered the lights are out permanently. Forget the panic and just focus for a moment on currency, our method of exchange. There is no Internet, there are no cell phones and the banks are closed: how do you buy and sell or feed your family? It seems impossible, but I can think of several scenarios that could cause this to happen: 1) a solar event (see Fox News: 1859 U.S., 1989 Canada, and 2003 space assets); 2) a terrorist attack with an electromagnetic pulse (EMP); and 3) natural disasters (earthquake, tsunami, etc.). It is estimated that the average community would be out of food in just three days. I am not a doomsayer, I am a scientist and such things are possible and therefore are worthy of consideration and planning. Remember, **THREE DAYS!**

The Essence of New Capital. Before we talk about New Capital, let's revisit Old Capital. In chapter 5, Collaborative Economics, we discussed (financial) capital as assets that can be invested and that without title an asset is hard to invest. Also, if you recall, Hernando De Soto said that assets without title are *"dead capital"* and unable to be multiplied into wealth. This can also be distinguished from capital (goods), which requires valuing human production in the process. For example, for a caveman, a stone or an arrowhead would be capital as they can be used to hunt or build something.

Any Discussions of New Capital Must Consider Valuing the Intangible with the Tangible. Traditionally, an intangible asset is defined as an item that has no physical presence. For example, a brand, a trademark, a patent, etc. These can be of huge value to a firm that produces products. An agreement may also be an intangible asset where it is classified as indefinite (meaning perpetual) or definite (meaning for a specified period). By contrast, a tangible asset is either a fixed asset (meaning a building, equipment, or land) or current asset (meaning a value such as inventory). If the tangible asset is held more than a year, for accounting purposes, it is depreciated according to an appropriate schedule.

So how do we turn tangible and intangible assets into New Capital? According to De Soto it takes "title." As we proceed in our discussion of Collaborative Economics, the desire is to be able to value the time, talent, or treasure of an individual as capital, but since people who have title (to them) are often thought of as slaves, this will require a new thinking on how to create such title. One way to think about it is this: **if you hold title to yourself, then you are not a slave, you are an investor.** This is a key to how collaboration will change society.

The Concept of Liquidity. Liquidity is one's ability to buy and sell an asset without affecting its price. Said another way, something liquid has the ability to be "exchanged" for currency in near real time, and this is also called marketability. Fixed assets are considered less liquid, since, for example, land or equipment, cannot be exchanged for currency as quickly as current assets like inventory can be.

Typically, a government issues "public currency" to provide immediate liquidity to its citizens, making money the most liquid of all assets. There are other forms of "private currency" such as public stock, BitCoins, points for air miles, discount coupons, script, etc., which will play a major role in the New Capital.

E. C. Reigel in his 1944 book entitled, *Private Enterprise Money- A Non-Political Money System* said, (page 6) ..."The first cardinal truth about money is that no one, individual or government, can issue money without buying something... The second cardinal truth is that money has to be backed by something, and the act of backing can only be the act of selling." He went on to say, (page 8) "Democratic government to date has been a pure illusion all that has been accomplished by voting or revolting is a change in the personnel of government." And lastly, he said, (page 8) " The first step toward political and economic freedom though the ultimate abolishment of the political money system is the establishing of the private non-political money system to demonstrate its feasibility." You can find this book for free on Google if you look it up by title. It is well worth it to read all 93 pages. One last quote, (page 11) " Therefore sovereignty of the people and democracy can be assured only if the people exercise their money power; and dictatorship in some form or another can be realized by the government's exercise of the money power." This is our alarm sounded. I had already conceived the Community Value Exchange System (CVES) when I found this book. Coincidence I think not!

The Community Value Exchange System (CVES). The CVES is where liquidity of assets takes place by establishing a currency equivalent for each asset. The closer the asset is to currency, the more liquid. Less liquid assets must consider time or discount as part of the calculation of their liquid value. This seems contradictory at first as assets in this class really define illiquid. However, if we create proper title, and achieve a proper discount for time and liquidity, we can value almost any time, talent, or treasure and exchange it into local currency in real time.

In December 2013, I spoke at the Future of Money and Technology Summit in San Francisco. My panel's topic was Community Crypt-Currency. For our purposes here, we'll call it "C³." This panel shared many ideas of how in the future, should the U.S. dollar or other global public currencies fail, new forms of value exchange would enable buying and selling of goods and services from the local community to a global marketplace.

To see the future, let's consider the past. In medieval times the king (the government) issued gold and silver coins. Gold was for wealth accumulation and silver was for the average person to exchange in the marketplace (like a dollar today). There was a limit to the amount of silver coins to be exchanged which created *scarcity* (re: Capitalism) and the more it was horded the more valuable it became.

So the merchants in the local village, who knew the *daily demand* (a timeframe) for their goods and services created a thing called *demand credits*. For demand credits to work there had to be a ready supply of merchants and consumers (buyers and sellers) within the community (the marketplace).

This system, often referred to as an *asset backed barter system*, worked as long as if I made shoes and you raised chickens we could trade (exchange) on an agreed value. But if I needed grain, then either the grain person had to agree to exchange with me for shoes, or we were at an impasse. This required that there be a system of trust or value exchange (a CVES). This usually began with a merchant with whom everyone did business (for example: bread) creating a *script voucher* that could be easily exchanged in the marketplace. (This is a great example of how coming from the extremes to the Commons solved the problem through reformation.) As merchants and consumers alike traded with this voucher for goods and services a new community currency was created backed by the underlying asset (bread) that everyone needed.

This *basis of value* is similar to the U.S. dollar today which is the world's reserve currency, based in what is called petro-dollars. The credit worthiness and ability to produce goods and services in demand made the dollar the natural choice. It has not always been that way; British Sterling once was the reserve currency. It might become the reserve currency again, as the credit worthiness of the United States is being degraded. All fiat (credit-backed) currency is at risk today. I believe we are headed to private community currency with a common value exchange, and if we lose electricity, it may have to degrade to local script! Forbes.com headlines a report in January 15, 2014, "… You Can Now Pay the IRS in Cryptocurrency;" and it is accurate, though payment must go through a third-party service provider for a fee. The day is coming soon that private Community Cryptocurrency (C³) will be as widely accepted and liquid as is public currency today. **A prediction: it is possible that soon (a decade or so) governments may be out of the currency business altogether, once sharing is fully integrated.** This was predicted by E.C. Reigel also.

So to finish this story of medieval times, as more and more merchants created their own script, there had to be a unit of measure so that the value exchange system could properly value (settle) the trades in either: 1) other script; 2) goods and services; or 3) the unit of measure (in those days – silver, today it might be the dollar).

I am working with a team of very bright people to develop a CVES, and we believe it will be able to exchange value for goods and services that are both tangible and intangible. This CVES will be private while at the same time be able to interface with the public liquidity (currency) system, and it will be able to clear transactions electronically, and will degrade to local script (C³) if we lose the Internet for a prolonged period of time. The scope of this book does not permit more detail of CVES, but if you want to know more about this part of Collaborative Commonwealth™ just make an inquiry to the website.

Collaborative Commonwealth™ - Business

The following three case studies should help us perceive how Collaborative Commonwealth™ might work within different business structures.

Case Study 1: Cooperative. For the last four years I have studied the changes in governance, in particular, the changes that have occurred in cooperative law in the state of Minnesota with their 308B Cooperative regulation as well in several other states. Minnesota is one of the national leaders in a new generation of CoOps that follow more of a limited liability company (LLC) structure as opposed to the more traditional C Corporation governance. I have helped several organizations follow this particular 308B design who are not domiciled in Minnesota, but use a registered agent and operate their CoOps in Texas, Idaho, Alabama, Tennessee, and Florida.

For this case study, I am citing a church organization in eastern Tennessee that operates a hydroponics greenhouse and sells to consumers in the local area. The 308B CoOps are allowed to have unlimited member classes. This particular group, the producer share class, agreed to contribute each $10,000 (in several payments), to purchase their one share and to have their one vote in the governance of the CoOp. This group has chosen to have a separate management agreement with a third-party since they learned the two reasons a CoOp typically fails are: 1) lack of capital; and 2) poor management by members.

These share members (the producers) will have the right to elect the Board of Directors from within the share class and as stated before will have one share/one vote each. Share members are eligible to pro-rata share in the profits, if any, that the CoOp earns. This is called a Patronage Refund (or Dividend).

They are following the Four Principles of Multiplication To Prosper In the Collaborative Economy from chapter 6 – *The Story Of The Teacher And The Student*.

Applying *Principle 1, The Principle of the Harvest*, they are planting seeds in two greenhouse quads (8 greenhouses total) on about one acre of land, using a multiplication system our team helped develop, where they can get the same growing power of about seven acres in a very small space. They can produce food year round from this facility.

Using *Principle 2: If You Don't Take A Risk, You Won't Multiply*, they used their best research and took a risk of capital to multiply a food source for their community.

They applied *Principle 3: The Principle of Excess – Investing with Others' Capital* and developed enough share members to pay cash for the project and they have a return of principal and interest plan for these share members.

And finally, they applied *Principle 4: The Principle of Gleaning or Caring for Others* and are sharing a portion of their first fruits with widows, orphans, the infirm, and the poor in their community.

Case Study 2: Collaborative Merchant Banking. Merchant Banking is a financing method that provides capital to companies in a form of share ownership instead of loans. Private merchant banks often provide advice on corporate matters to the firms they assist with finances. Merchant banks are in fact the original banks. Invented in the Middle Ages by Italian grain merchants, they are about managing trade.

Today, small businesses that have the potential to grow quickly by selling large quantities of goods or services cannot obtain traditional bank loans. They are looking for Collaborative Merchant Banking to help support this growth. This type of finance is also called arbitrage, factoring, forfeiting, consignment, peer-to-peer lending, and crowd funding. The largest retailers and home improvement companies use these financial methods to compete globally. They have become experts at managing payment terms.

Let's say that a manufacturer wants to offer a retailer "net 90" terms (meaning you can pay your invoice anytime within 90 days with no late fees). Second, your store can sell this product or service in 30 days (this is the velocity component). This means you can sell it before you have to pay for it (this is leverage or multiplication aspect). However, there is a catch. You have to have the assets to prove to the manufacturer, that you can pay in 90 days whether you sell it or not. This is where Collaborative Merchant Banking comes in and shares this risk by providing capital to guarantee this payment. It is a calculated risk. (Remember Principle 2: If You Don't Take A Risk, You Won't Multiply).

Example, I have a friend who is a pilot and can earn up to $14,000 for flying much needed parts from point A to point B in a few hours. This *hot shot* freight pays a high price because if an assembly line is down, and they need a part to fix it, $14,000 is cheap compared to loss of production for hours or even days. Literally this happens daily all over the country as manufacturers keep fewer and fewer parts on-hand to reduce costs. The pilot spent all his money buying the airplane, but still needs money for fuel, maintenance, etc.

His financial statement was used to buy the plane; he cannot reuse it to borrow extra money from a traditional bank with the same balance sheet. He will gladly pay 5 to 10% of his invoice to have access to this cash today; otherwise he loses the opportunity to earn the $14,000 income. (This is opportunity cost or risk)

As a Collaborative Merchant Banker you could enter into an agreement with the pilot to provide for his expenses, maybe be partners, and share in this transaction. Let's say he can fly these flights at $10,000 daily, but he cannot collect for 60 days, and let's say each flight costs $5,000 in expenses. Looking at the numbers, if he flies 20 days a month X $5,000 he will need $100,000 a month in working capital X 2 months. To get paid he will need $200,000 in working capital. That is 40 invoices at $10,000 each or about $400,000 in account receivables. If as a Collaborative Merchant Bank I could earn 5% that would be $20,000 ($400,000 X 5%) in 60 days on my $200,000 at risk. So if I did this for a year, I would have earned $120,000 (6 X $20,000) for my $200,000 at risk or a 60% return. The pilot's clients are big companies that always pay; they just pay on their terms (in 60 days). This is a calculated risk that can earn 60% a year!   By sharing, the money goes to the collaborators, not traditional bankers.

I know of transactions where the money is made daily (for example private ATM Vault Cash). Also there are businesses where the turnover (velocity) is greater such that sales can be made multiple times within a 30 day period and the yields exceed 60% on the capital. I hope you see the opportunity in collaborative trade finance. Sharing is the future of finance.

Suppose that there are 10 people who come together to collaborate as merchant bankers and want to use their IRA funds collectively at $500,000. They might form as a multi-member LLC, a corporation, a cooperative, or as shareholders of preferred shares in a collaborative public company. If they can earn 30 to 100% annually, and they can do it tax free in their Roth IRA, this makes more sense than giving it to a traditional bank that pays 1 to 2%

and keeps the rest! Really, what if it was just 10%, remember the Rule of 72's! Let's assume they could earn 2% at the bank, so it would take 36 years to double. If they earned 10% it would take 7.2 years to double and if the low of 30% it would double in 2.4 years! So if there was 36 years to retire you would have $50,000 X 2 or $100,000 per person at the bank. But with the merchant banking concept you get 15 doubles: 1: 50 to 100, 2: 100 to 200... 15: that's $819,200,000 each! Hard to believe, but that is why banks have marble and you have vinyl floors!

In the 21st century, I predict there will be numerous groups that use this strategy to earn income for themselves and grow our economy at the same time. There are thousands of these kind of transactions in almost every industry just waiting for agile collaborators to step in and receive their "pro-rata share" of the profits with the buyer and seller. **Again, before jumping into an agreement, consult with your attorney, CPA, or financial advisor so that you comply with all the securities and tax laws.**

Case Study 3: Collaborative Public Company. For the last eighteen months, I have worked with the management of microcap public companies to reform their articles, bylaws, and agreements such that they would utilize Collaborative Commonwealth™ governance. Instead of the Imperial CEO, they had to commit a leadership strategy into two parts: 1) *Administrative servant officers* (much like the management company in Case Study 1: Cooperative); and 2) a Board of Advisors each who *are the operators* of the underlying subsidiaries.

They utilize a traditional Board of Directors to establish governance and set policy.

Because of the structure, **they share the consolidated financial statements** and are able to consolidate gross income and assets. This blending of income and assets will make a very favorable impression on shareholders and lenders alike. Each subsidiary is in its own Preferred Share Class and as such each business may, with the Board's approval, declare a qualified dividend which will help shareholders and operators of the subsidiaries save on ordinary income tax. The Preferred Shares have two features which make them very attractive: 1) an excellent conversion ratio to common stock, which provides for liquidity; and 2) a Lockup Leak-out Agreement to protect all shareholders from any one dumping the shares or shorting the stock, which is a form of asset protection.

Suffice it to say; these features which are similar to the CoOp advantages but are increased by the leverage of a public company are making history in how collaboration and pro-rata sharing are far superior to competition and scarcity. The key here is they are both making a profit! One company expects to increase its net worth by at least $50 Million in the first 18 months.

Thought Mastery

With the CHANGE coming, we need reformation.

What caused the Occupy Movement to fail was a lack of Leadership Emergence. It allowed outside factions to use propaganda to pick their ideals apart.

Our current governance system is broken. We need reformation. We've got to stop the crisis of fear brought on by scarcity, and we have to control our purse strings (entitlements). You can't borrow yourself out of debt!

Social Media has proven it is the way to reach literally billions of people as in the case of Facebook®.

Any future aspect of global planning, must consider:
1) social networks/circles
2) electronic commerce, and
3) the multicultural aspects of this collaboration

The financial impact of this group uniting as a consumer organization, would control not only the majority of goods and services, but could declare its own community currency.

Translating this to a business environment, where governance is important, and there is commerce and exchange between producers and consumers. They relate through commerce, but they do not attempt to govern each other. Instead, they operate by contract (covenant or agreement) where all parties can reach "mutual assent" on how the project will be achieved and how each will be compensated according to their pro-rata value exchange. Future governance will be more virtual and operate by agreements (See chapter 8).

There will need to be created a better system. I call it the **Community Value Exchange System (CVES)**, this is were liquidity of assets takes place by establishing a currency-equivalent for each asset. A community crypto-currency (C^3) may be the answer. This currency must be able to degrade so that in the event of a technology disaster where we lost connectivity or even computers, we could still provide goods and services in the local marketplace by the use of script.

CHAPTER 8 – FRAMISDORTIN

You Do Know The World Has Changed!

Throughout this book we have talked about change and reformation, I have asked, "Are you ready to be a change agent?" A friend sent me a very interesting (private) video done by a direct sales company about the concept of *The Connected Economy*. Here are my thoughts about that video.

In 1917, the Smith-Hughes Act was written to help our nation face a problem. If we were to compete in the industrial economy we had to overcome a shortage. Our shortage was not natural resources; it was who would be the obedient factory workers. This is why the public school system was expanded. It taught our children to show up on time, follow a schedule, listen to a leader, respond to a ringing bell, and in general convert a nation of dreamers into a nation of factory workers. It worked! Also in 1917, the National Education Association was created. Coincidence?

For nearly 80 years (a life cycle) we bought into the dream of being an employee for a big company that would pay us enough so we wouldn't quit and we would work hard enough so we wouldn't get fired, and if all that worked you would retire and get a gold watch! This was the story of my parents. They were referred to as the Greatest Generation.

By 1997, this generation had begun to pass away and the Baby-boomers, my generation, started to inherit the world (we were maturing into our most productive time (30's to 40's) in our 80 year life cycle. The industrial revolution was fading and the technology revolution was emerging. It was before dot-com went dot-bomb. My generation fulfilled the expectations of our parents and was forced to make the change to use technology in business.

The children of the Baby-boomers, the Millennials and Gen X are the beginning of the New Great Generation. They still work in factories of paper and technology, are paying dearly for that precious college education, and often can't find a job; but they will lead the way to the Collaborative Economy. I will be 80 in 2035, my sons will be as I am now, in their mid 50's and their children will be in their late 20's to mid-30's. This is the overlapping 40 and 80 year life cycles I discussed before. This is what causes economies to rise and fall – not what most people think. If you plot all of this data on a typical S curve, you will find it was expected that the economy would crash in about 2008 and not recover until about 2023 (reference economist Harry S. Dent, Jr.). The technology revolution has emerged strong, right on time, as my children now enter their 30's. This change is predicable!

Back to the story…Looking back 250 years (a great economic cycle according to Tytler, Marx and others) there are more people on Facebook® today (1.1 billion) than were in the world in the mid to late 1700's (about 700 million according to About.com). The Millennials are the first collaborators (they know how to connect globally using technology). If they embrace what I am proposing in this chapter, my grandchildren will walk into their 30's in a new world (with between 8 and 9 billion people) that looks nothing like the industrial economy with its two opposing forces of capitalism and socialism. It will be a unified economy, connected and collaborating globally through technology like smart phones, tablets, and computers. In fact, most money will be in a new wallet called the smart telephone, paper and coin as currency will be part of the history books.

The education system will have changed from an industrial structure with a hierarchical method designed to produce degreed workers to Massive Open Online Courses (MOOCs) producing skill-specific, visionary, out-of-the-box thinkers who apply open source technology to connect and collaborate. I predict, we will **"grow globally, locally"** by becoming agile communities connected in an EcoSphere Confederation (see chapter 9) using Collaborative Commonwealth™.

My grandchildren, the new 30-Something's (about 2035 or about a decade after the recovery), will be the New Great Generation of "collaborateurs" (collaborative entrepreneurs). Each person will own their intangible and tangible value, likely as their own personal company. They will not be employees, but will be collaborators in many projects according to their gifting and purpose in life.

However, **the change can be today, not in the future**. The Millennials will lead the way financed by the Baby-boomers, and next generation (our grandchildren) will prosper from it.

The question is, what will this new work environment look like?

My NASA Story

I was very privileged to be apart of the NASA Space Shuttle Program from the very first shuttle flight back in 1981. My role was in assent and powered flight design for the first and second stage propulsion, aborts, and training astronauts on the remote manipulator system (RMS) called *the arm*. Yes, I know, it doesn't take a rocket scientist, but in those days, I was one.

While I was at NASA, I had the opportunity to participate in thought leadership and work along side some of the greatest minds our country had to offer. When we needed to solve a problem or figure out an interface (how to connect something), the German scientists in our group would say, "What we need is a *framisdortin!*" It was their slang word for the fix or interface. Over the years, I have never forgotten that term and I with honor and affection have included it in my design of Collaborative Commonwealth™ to describe the virtual interface (connecting) structure for the next generation of corporate governance designs.

In this chapter, I will show how each collaborator will connect with the world using the Framisdortin as an open-handed universal interface (bus) where business and the reformed businesses and governments can collaborate for the benefit of society, shareholders, collaborators, and customers (consumers).

Every Individual Will Be A Company

I shared earlier a quote from a friend and engineer named Dan Robles. Dan is one of the pioneers for change to a collaborative economic system, and he believes that in the future, every individual will become a corporation. I agree that individuals should each personally incorporate and many may choose to become an LLC instead. Either will work. As we move toward Collaboratism as an economic system this will be the trend. Corporate America is already downsizing, removing benefits, soon consultants and independent contractors will be the norm.

Top down command and control that is vertically integrated requires huge capitalization and is fragile by nature; whereas, collaborative pro-rata sharing using circular open architecture requires less capital, is agile, and allows individual entrepreneurs, *collaborateurs*, to emerge following the concept of water: Drops, Streams, Rivers, and Oceans. It is shared assets, not invested assets, which will build a new economic system.

Jeremy Rifkin, a well known economist, in his book entitled *The Zero Marginal Cost Society*, in chapter 6, citing Mahatma Gandhi's view of "not mass production, but production by the masses" talks about a move from an industrial world (capitalism) to a new economic order that moves away from mass production (with its vertically integrated enterprises and inherent tendencies toward centralized economic power and monopolized markets) to local production by the masses in their own communities. Ghandi called this "Swadeshi." Gandhi said about *Swadeshi*, "My idea of village Swaraj (self governance) is that it is a complete republic (a commonwealth), independent of its neighborhoods for its own vital wants, and yet interdependent for many others which dependence is a necessity." Gandhi continued to discuss the notion of pyramidically organized society in contrast to what he called *oceanic circles* made up of communities of individuals (I suggest, "collaborateurs"). Again coincidence, I think not.

The idea that every community must be self sustaining (think CVES from chapter 7) and interconnected with other communities is a global thought that must emerge. As I read this idea in comparison with my thoughts expressed in the concept of water (chapter 1), over 70 years ago, Gandhi saw the same idea from a different view. **This ultimately creates an environment where** collaborateurs form business ventures using open-source agreements to share intellectual property, which I call the *Framisdortin* (the interface or the connector).

The New Resume

Again, Dan Robles, has been working on an idea he calls "Curiosume," a new form of resume. Dan postulates that the best non-competitive paring (sharing) is teacher/student. In Dan's way of thinking, and I agree with him, the resume as we know it today is obsolete. In fact, it is possible that in the very near future the degree system used by colleges and universities, as we know it, will pass in favor or shared knowledge among community peer sets, possibly taught through collaborative MOOCs. **This will be the reformation of the education system.**

In Dan's model, Ingenesist.com, some of the features of Curiosume are:

- No competition – removes incentive to cheat
- Anonymous until point of transaction (privacy) where the true identity can be revealed
- Can display different personas to the marketplace as a function of position or role being applied for
- Personal API allows users to *"own"* their data
- Geo-matching allows for community projects
- Matches supply and demand
- Values tangible and intangible assets
- Allows for smart contracts with cryptographic keys
- Provides engagement and gaming functions

- Shuts out Big Data unless they "pay a toll" to access it
- Wiki provides a global standard definition of interests with graphing capability of individual talents

Clearly, this new open source paring using three sigmas (σ) of deviation from a collaborative norm for each the teacher and the student can facilitate the knowledge and interest paring needed by the Framisdortin.

The idea of Framisdortin is that it is the virtual interface, a governance model (agreement), whereby individuals (Drops) can be aligned in to Steams, merged into Rivers or create potential in Oceans as the Collaborative Economy develops.

Concept Collaboration

William H. Davidow states in his book, *The Virtual Corporation*,

> By the year 2015, the United States will either be a leader in this new business revolution or it will be a postindustrial version of a developing country. Either a nation of independent knowledge workers or a colony of economic serfs. It will either enjoy a high standard of living or suffer increasing impoverishment – it will be either an economy transformed or a graveyard of industrial skeletons (1992, p. 2).

The idea of individuals, groups, or companies coming together to work on a concept or product is not new, and it is an idea whose time is emerging.

The question is, "How will all these independent thinkers, absent of a leader, work together to produce anything?" That is precisely the point. In this book, I have shared a great number of ideas, chapter by chapter.

- First, how people come together (connect).
- Next, the need for leadership emergence and the building blocks of new governance.
- Then, the next chapters examined key principles, made comparisons of what the new order looks like and what it is not, and gave examples of how it is being applied;
- But now, how we take it to the ultimate organization structure may be the most important part.

It will take unity and enough social dissatisfaction with status quo to effect change. Pro-rata sharing is at the core of this concept; When we:

- **can value human time, talent, and treasure (like Curiosume);**
- **exchange that value as liquid currency (like CVES);**
- **are connected by technology and agreement (the Framisdortin);**
- **and have an EcoSystem Confederation (chapter 9).**

We will have the governance model for a new Collaborative Economic System called Collaborative Commonwealth™. It will emerge agile and ready for the next 250 year cycle of economic growth where individuals (Drops) are rewarded and valued; where products, services, concepts, can pro-rata share profits; and where EcoSystems (Oceans) can emerge and thrive.

Concepts in Framisdortin Agreement

According to Black's Law Dictionary, the definition of an agreement is (http://thelawdictionary.org/agreement/),

A concord of understanding and intention, between two or more parties, with respect to the effect upon the irrelative rights and duties, of certain past or future facts or performances. The act of two or more persons, who unite in expressing a mutual and common purpose, with the view of altering their rights and obligations. A coming together of parties in opinion or determination; the union of two or more minds in a thing done or to be done; a mutual assent to do a thing. Com. Dig. 'Agreement,' A 1. The consent of two or more persons concurring, the one in parting with, the other in receiving, some property, right, or benefit. Bac. Abr. A promise, or undertaking. This is a loose and incorrect sense of the word. Wain v. Warlters. 5 East. 11. The writing or instrument which is evidence of an agreement. Agreements are of the following several descriptions, viz.: Conditional agreements, the operation and effect of which depend upon the existence of a supposed state of facts, or the performance of a condition, or the happening of a contingency. Executed agreements, which have reference to past events, or which are at once closed and where nothing further remains to be done by the parties. Executory agreements are such as are to be performed in the future. They are commonly preliminary to other more formal or important contracts or deeds, and are usually evidenced by memoranda, parol promises, etc. Express agreements are those in which the terms and stipulations are specifically declared and avowed by the parties at the time of making the agreement.

Translated, an agreement is where two or more parties reach mutual assent as to consideration (payment), terms and conditions (performance), a timeframe (period), and an outcome (production). In future contract law, the Framisdortin Agreement must act also as the connector or interface. Traditionally, except by joint venture, one of the entities is asking another entity to perform, with its employees, a task. In joint venture, both parties have come together for a purpose and when that purpose is complete the agreement terminates. This is the business of the future, purposed and agile.

The Framisdortin Agreement finds its roots in joint venture. The exception is that we wish to avoid the individual liability associated with partnership where the parties are joint and several liable for the acts or omissions of the other partner. Another common word for such agreement might be strategic alliance. This is why in the future everyone is a company. The governance forms a corporation or limited liability company. The kind does not matter as long as it affords limited liability to the stakeholders or members respectively.

If you recall in the chapter 7 case studies, we talked about the Collaborative Public Company. In this example, the company created new governance, based on Collaborative Commonwealth™ principles, and then by structure of an Acquisition Agreement and reformed bylaws, created unlimited Preferred Share Classes as its means of joining the company and its subsidiaries into one common balance sheet and income statement. This kind of structure enables a company to become an EcoSystem or EcoSystem Confederation where each company maintains its own identity, soul, rights, as with a Drop. Several might align as a Stream, by possibly forming intra-company alliances. Drops or Streams may connect by agreement with outside companies in an inter-company arrangement like joint venture or strategic alliances. The options are endless.

In either case, pro-rata sharing of value, assets, income, and expenses should be apart of the agreements from the beginning.

To cover all the possibilities of Framisdortin Agreements is outside the scope of this book. In fact, it is an entire business advisory practice. My company, SPECTRUM Advanced Markets, Inc. (www.spectrumadvancedmarkets.com), currently provides this service to select clients.

Thought Mastery

Are you ready to become a CHANGE AGENT?

Do you have a grasp on the 20, 40, 80, and 250 year cycles that impact our economy?

What is your plan if we have another economic crisis between 2014 and 2023. According to numerous economic experts it is not if, but when. Dent, says the economy won't recover until 2023 based on the generational spending in the 20, 40, and 80 year cycles. What is your plan? Survival or Multiplication?

Have you looked into Massive Open Online Courses (MOOCs). You may need to increase your skills in several areas, why not start today?

Do you embrace "Every Individual Will Be A Company?" If so, what is your company going to be able to contribute? Where are your fellow Streams, Rivers, or Oceans you need to connect. Have you started to create your "New Resume" for the Collaborative Economy?

Davidow, in *The Virtual Corporation*, said by 2015 the US will either be a leader in the new economy or be a postindustrial version of a developing country. How do you plan to collaborate in the future?

Do you know where you will connect, where is your Framisdortin?

It will take unity and enough social dissatisfaction with status quo to effect change. Pro-rata sharing is at the core of this concept. When we value human time, talent, and treasure (like Curiosume), exchange that value as liquid currency (like CVES), are connected by technology and agreement (like Framisdortin), and have EcoSystem Confederation (chapter 9), we will have the governance model for a new Collaborative Economic System called Collaborative Commonwealth™. It will emerge agile and ready for the next 250 year cycle of economic growth where individuals (Drops) are rewarded and valued; where products, services, concepts, can pro-rata share profits; and where EcoSystems (Oceans) can emerge and thrive.

Chapter 9 – EcoSystem Confederation

If you recall in The Concept of Water, we developed the concept of the community Economic System (EcoSystem). We also referred to an EcoSystem as a body of water, a potential, and a reservoir of collaborative knowledge.

Collaborative Commonwealth™ as a form of governance is not Federal, Democratic, Capitalist, or Socialist; it is Collabortist. However, this does not mean that it is to the exclusion of societal or governmental structure (it is not Anarchist either). Anarchy or Anarchism is a hierarchy-free, self-governing system that does not use a central governance model. By contrast, Collaborative Commonwealth™ (an EcoSystem) does have a negotiated central governance core like a Republic or Commonwealth that allows for even a higher order of Confederation between EcoSystems to form an EcoSphere. It also provides for a lower order of governance, all the way to an individual (a Drop) and all elements between.

There is a distinct order in how it interrelates within and without and how it generates and shares a profit pro-rata with all members according to their value invested.

If you recall our earlier discussions about movements, how the next reformation or revolution often maintains a remnant the former system, Collaborative Commonwealth™, or the EcoSystem (economic system), does not throw out all aspects of former economic systems. Collaborative Commonwealth™ retains and embodies the best practices of previous governance. For example:

- We keep most of the Republic
- We keep most of Commonwealth
- We discard much of Democracy
- We keep earning a profit from Capitalism and make it better with pro-rata profit sharing as in CoOp.
- We keep helping the poor from Socialism, but we made it a community responsibility not a government entitlement
- We keep the idea of the commons from Communism and tossed the rest.
- We do not use Federal

We choose the preferred Confederate model which gives us liberty by actual association or alliance but allowed separation if a unit disagrees with the whole (true freedom).

Confederation is not just a southern United States historical ideal; it is a proven global governance concept. *Confederacy* is defined as a union, league, or alliance of sovereign units (Drops, Streams, Rivers, and Oceans) for common action in relation to other units.

The units are created by treaty (agreement) and may emerge into a constitution (articles of incorporation or organization with bylaws and agreements) with **the central elected governance acting as servants in a support role**. The specific versions to consider also allow for secession (the ability to exercise your free will and leave the collaboration). In its non-political context, a confederation is used to describe an organization that consolidates leadership and authority only to provide unity and clear direction of a common purpose. It promotes best practices learned from real life experiences.

In Collaborative Commonwealth™, each unit contractually leaves an eyelet (or plug, or connector) within each entity that allows a Framisdortin Agreement to connect each element required in a confederation such that each can be drawn together as in a draw string bag and operate as one for a common purpose.

Borrowing from new generation CoOp thinking, each unit will have pro-rata revenue shares or share benefits (similar to Patronage Refunds or Patronage Dividends) according to its production and value exchanged to the entire organizational effort. **Basically, no work – no pay, fair and proportional.**

This concept of revenue sharing (sometimes known as patronage) is different from commissions and share ownership. For example if likened to commissions, the person is compensated based solely on a completed transaction independent of profit or costs. If I am a shareholder, I revenue share only if there is a profit and only if management chooses to share with me. Even worse if I am an employee, I am paid a fixed amount which likely has nothing to do with the success of the venture. **As an owner of a revenue share, I have both reward and risk since I am a collaborator.**

This structure can also be applied to the gathering together of people, systems, structures, networks, and EcoSystems allowing each element its own independence while creating interdependence among the units for a season of time. It springs forth from a concept of tribes.

I would like to share some quotes from Seth Godin's widely read book, *Tribes – We Need You to Lead Us.*

- "You can't have a tribe without a leader and you can't be a leader without a tribe" (p.2).
- "We want to belong not to just one tribe, it turns out but to many tribes and if you give us the tools and make it easy we will keep joining other tribes" (p. 3).
- "Tribes are about faith – about belief in an idea and in the community" (p. 9).
- "Most of all we're stuck acting like managers or employees instead of like the leaders we could become by embracing the factory instead of the tribe" (p.10).
- "It turns out the people who lack jobs the most also are the ones who are doing the best work making the greatest impact and changing the most" (p. 11).
- "Leadership is about creating change that you believe in."(p. 14).

In just the first few pages of Godin's little book, wisdom abounds. It is good to be the king, but to be the king you have to have a kingdom. The idea is that each individual needs to be their own company (kingdom), and then you have rights to connect to a tribe, a Stream, a River, and Ocean, whatever you want to call it. When, Martin Luther King Jr. gave his "I Have A Dream" speech, it started a movement of whites and blacks because it was their dream too. Belief, calling, purpose, leadership, economics, a plan, vision, or dream, this is what brings about change. Is this you? It is the *why*, not the *what*. Status quo is no longer the way to go. Change is the way to go. It seems that we are all rushing toward the new idea and the established thing is no longer the popular idea.

Let's consider just a few more quotes from Tribes.

- "People yearn for change, relish being a part of the movement, and they talk about things that are remarkable, not boring"(p. 18).
- "Managers manage by using the authority the factory gives them. You listened to your manager or you lose your job. A manager can't make change because that is not his job. His job is to complete task assigned to him or someone else in the factory... Leaders, on the other hand, don't care very much for organizational structure or the official blessing of whatever factory they work for. They use passion and ideas to lead people, as opposed to using threats and bureaucracy to manage them. Leaders must become aware of how the organization (governance) works because this awareness allows them to change it" (p.22).

I will let you purchase the book and read the rest of what Seth Godin has to share. It is worth the read if you intend to be a leader in the Collaborative Movement. Like *Collaborative Commonwealth*, it is a small book and very easy to read. One last quote from the back cover, "If you think leadership is only for other people, you're wrong. We need YOU to lead us." We definitely need leaders in this movement, will you accept the call?

People

For our purposes, people (or Drops) are the most critical component of an EcoSystem as they are the users, producers, leaders, or activators. They make stuff happen. They stir a need for there to be an Economic System. In economics, the value exchange or transaction can be simply stated as the buyer and seller (relational and competitive). In chapter 8 – The Framisdortin, we learned there are other relationships like "student and teacher" that are not so transactional in nature but are more relational and collaborative in nature. They are equally important to the environment of how communities are built in how they intra-act and inter-act with each other.

While leadership is important, it is collaboration with the first followers as equals that makes a movement a success.

Systems

Within an EcoSystem, there are independent systems which perform functions that are either stand alone or components (subsystems) of other larger systems. A system can be defined as ordered and comprehensive assemblage of facts, principals, rules, doctrines, logical steps, in a unified field of knowledge, or expertise (an alignment). It is the same as Streams in chapter 1.

Structure

A structure is an order or alignment of things or systems to accomplish a purpose unto itself or in conjunction with other elements of the EcoSystem. It is a gatherer or connector of systems (a collaboration). The same as Rivers in chapter 1.

Networks

Networks represent an interrelated collection of people, systems, and structures that create connectivity (potential). Like nerves in a body, they connect all the parts so they can work together. The same as a body of water (lake, sea, or ocean) with potential as in chapter 1.

EcoSystem

An EcoSystem is the universe of connected networks within a defined region: community, city, state, country. It represents the economic system of that region. In Collaborative Commonwealth™ it operates as a confederacy. This can be likened to multiplied potential.

EcoSpheres

An EcoSphere is the universe of connected EcoSystems. If you liken an EcoSystem to a community, then an EcoSphere represents a niche channel, or even a global community. This can be likened to geometric potential.

Thought Mastery

Collaborative Commonwealth™ as a form of governance is not Federal, Democratic, Capitalist, or Socialist; it is Confederate, balanced by open pro-rata sharing, and Collabortist in nature.

If you recall how often the next reformation or revolution maintains a remnant the former system; Collaborative Commonwealth™ or the EcoSystem (economic system), does not throw out all aspects of the former economic systems. In fact, I believe we have retained the best practices of governance and embodied them into Collaborative Commonwealth™.

Confederation is not just a southern United States historical ideal; it is defined as a union, league, or alliance of sovereign units (Drops, Steams, Rivers, and Oceans) for common action in relation to other units.

This concept of revenue sharing (sometimes know as patronage) is different from commissions and share ownership.

Re-read all the quotes from Seth Godin in this chapter.

Where do you connect right now? Is it with other individuals, with systems, with structures, with networks, or with an EcoSystem? It could be multiple places. Write your thoughts in your journal.

Chapter 10 – The Assessment, Patching Your Holes

My wife, Cheryl-Ann, worked as an Organization Development Consultant in the corporate sector, so I asked her for ideas for this chapter. Much of the material in this chapter comes from one or more of my books and from her book *Sound Alignment*.

Since Drops align with other Drops to form a Stream and that is the basic building block of the Collaborative Movement, first we need to assess ourselves and learn to assess others. Bad alignments create scars and often kill dreams. When this happens, momentum is broken, and it is hard to recover.

Assessment 1: Desire and Action

In almost every book I have written, I have included the **Desire/Action Window** because it is fundamental in understanding yourself and others.

The Desire/Action Window. Take a few minutes and review the model which follows and see where you fit.

	DESIRE	desire
ACTION	I	II
action	III	IV

ACTION = puts forth lots of action
action = fails to act, always
DESIRE = has lots of desire
desire = has lower desire

Are you a Type I (Big D – Big A)? These people have a burning DESIRE to achieve their purpose. They are willing to maximize their ACTION; they have learned that you only achieve results by doing. They will invest their time, treasure, talent, and avoid indecision at all costs. Is this you?

Are you a Type II (Little d – Big A)? These people are faithful to a cause, they follow a plan. They are willing to do the work and take ACTION. They work each assignment every day and they usually leave the development of the plan to others who are more experienced. They believe that this "thing" works and simply trust it. However, somewhere along the way, their desire (dreams) got crushed by some circumstance and today they believe others win, but likely, I won't. So unlike Type I, they are lower on desire. Is this you?

Are you a Type III (Big D – Little a)? These people dream of what it will be like when someday they will achieve all their dreams and often they DESIRE to own and operate their own small business. Sometimes, they are so excited that they will say, "I get the plan, let's do it!" But when it comes to follow through and taking action, they seem to fall short. Type III's exhibit a lot of DESIRE, but fall short on action. Is this you?

Are you a Type IV (Little d – Little a)? These people want someone else to come up with the plan, so they just don't have to think about it. They would rather someone else do the work to, so they can just get credit for it (this is the byproduct of the industrial/factory mindset). Their desire is, "when will we get our next day off" and their action is, "can we put this off until next week, my back hurts, the sun's in my eyes, I need a break before we start, the football game is on during that time, etc." They invent any excuse for distraction. However, they are first in line for the paycheck. Is this you?

Which Type Were You?

If you are a Type I you are a leader, a winner, and I pray you join this movement. The movement needs you!

If you are a Type II, you are a hard worker, and you get things done. We just need to get you re-inspired and you will be a great leader or team member. The movement needs you!

If you are a Type III, you are a dreamer. It is not hard for you to "talk the talk" but you rarely "walk the walk." Dreamers almost never escape where they are today. They are great people to be around; they are almost always positive people. Likely, unless you can reform your thinking and change your belief system, you will be a late comer to the Collaborative Movement. There is hope, but you've got to change, overcome your fear of taking Action and get someone to hold you accountable. You will struggle with this accountability as you do not see yourself the way others see you, but if you change, you could win. My experience tells me the odds are 80:20 you won't change; this is also called Pareto's principle.

If you are a Type IV, you are not going to succeed, I am sorry. In fact in the Tytler quote you are moving toward dependency. Your life will get worse and worse, yet you won't do anything about it. For you to succeed, it will take what is called by psychiatrist a Significant Emotional Event (a SEE). Only about 10% of people who get cancer, heart disease, or are financially broke change, the rest fail. You likely are in the 97% that will retire dead...dead broke and dependent on a government.

You cannot "fake it until you make it."

It is not important where you have been

It is only important where you are going

Assessment 2: Take A Few Tests

The first is a personality test such as Meyers-Briggs®. There are 16 personality combinations, which one are you? What are your best team mates? Who are the best people to marry? There are many providers of this type of test. I found one for free. www.16personalities.com.

Next, is called a DISC which is another personality test. Again, there are a wide range of combinations, which one are you? What are your best team mates? Who are the best people to marry? There are many providers of this type of test, I found one for free that I suggest you start with. It can be found at www. discpersonalitytesting.com.

The last test is a strengths test. I recommend either, StrengthsFinder 2.0 which may cost you about $20 to purchase an online code, or The Merit Profile™ costs a bit more but it provides more information personally and on team building.

Assessment 3: Distractions

This is a true statement, "All distractions are equal!" If what distracts you distracts you, then it doesn't matter what it is. Over the years, I have taught a basic formula called The Dream Equation.

$$\text{Wealth (Dreams)} = \text{Capital (Vehicle)} \times \frac{[(T1+T2+T3)]}{\text{Distractions}}$$

T1= Time, T2 = Talent, and T3= Treasure

To obtain Wealth or Dreams, first you need either Capital or a Vehicle. A Vehicle could be a business, a job, an investment, a strategy, etc. What is interesting is that whatever you choose is multiplied by a fraction. In elementary school we learned that if we multiply times a fraction, we get less than we started with. So clearly here Distractions are dream thieves. **To maximize your future, you have to minimize your distractions.**

In your journal, write down all your known distractions and what steps you can take to remove them from your life.

Assessment 4: Patching Your Ship

Cheryl-Ann and I refer to our Vehicles as "Ships." We have learned over time that without proper planning, if we send out 10 ships, 8 will likely sink or be lost due to environmental risks, poor planning, or lack of funding. The remaining 2 may return with treasure, unless there are pirates, and often there are pirates who come into your business as distractions or bad alignments.

Before setting sail on you adventure, you need to assess your ship. Most of us have a dream or goal. These are the sails of your ship. Wind is a necessary unseen hand/force. If you remember in "Chapter 2- Leadership Emergence" I recounted the story of Noah and the Ark. In this example, the ship was the Ark (the natural thing). The unseen hand of the wind was that God sent two things, the animals and the flood (the supernatural things). I don't care what your belief system is, but you have to believe in something more than yourself. If you do that, then that which you believe is the wind in your sails. No wind, no trip unless you want to row the whole way. That is taking the hard way to your purpose.

In addition to the sails, your Hull (the body of the ship) has to be sea worthy (ready for the trip). We have identified many holes that you need to inspect your ship and if you have them, repair them before your journey. Here are three:

Hole 1: Sound Alignment. You have to make sure that you build your connections, team, crew, joint venturers, etc. with the people you need, not necessarily the people you most like. Divorce in marriage and in business can be costly in money, relationships, and time! Use Assessments 1 and 2 to help you evaluate your team. Choosing relationships wisely saves time and money and therefore increases profit.

Hole 2: Honor. It is important that you build your relationships and business with integrity and honor. If you sign an agreement, perform on that agreement. If you promise to pay, then pay on time. It is like the Principle of the Harvest we discussed, "Seed replicates after its own kind;" if you sew honor you will reap honor. If you sow dishonor, you will reap what you sow (dishonor). Honoring, builds trust and trust is essential in relationships, connections, and collaboration.

Hole 3: Focus. Knowing who you are and not pretending to be more or less than you are is essential. Lying about your skills, your abilities, your experience will catch up with you. It goes to character and reputation. Character is who you are independent of others; reputation is who others say you are. The objective here is to know your focus, your role. Sometimes you need to lead, sometimes you need to follow, and sometimes you need to just rest and be quiet.

Assessing your hull, and plugging your holes will expedite your journey to success. **Even a great wind (belief system or movement) can't push a sinking ship very far. This is wisdom, learn it.**

Thought Mastery

Have you decided to engage and become involved? Will you emerge as a leader?

From Assessment 1, which type are you?

From Assessment 2, What is your Meyers-Briggs ® four letter personality designation. Did you read the detailed report to understand how you work and interrelate (connect) with others? What was your DISC profile? Which did you choose StengthsFinder or The Merit Profile™? Do you know how to find others who might be a "Sound Alignment" for your team?

From Assessment 3, have you made your list of distractions? Remember to maximize your future; you must minimize your distractions.

From Assessment 4, How many holes did you have? Remember, if you don't patch the hull, you leak and your ship cannot get to its destination no matter how much wind you have in your sails.

CHAPTER 11 – FINDING YOUR PLACE

This is really the final chapter of this book, since chapter 12 is a summary of all the Thought Mastery from each chapter to facilitate a quick reference to all the lessons learned in the book.

I truly struggled with what to say to you at the end of this book. The reason is that there is so much ahead in Collaborative Commonwealth™ that is to yet be discovered or revealed. This is not the end but the beginning. There will be other thought leaders, innovators, and Collaborateurs who read this book and then launch into projects in all four governance realms: Government, For-Profit, Non-Profit and Cooperative.

You, The Drop, The Beginning

I trust that you have made frank and accurate journal entries as you have read this book. If you skipped that point, may I suggest that you start over and do the homework. Collaborative Commonwealth™ is not hard, complicated, or even really all that different from what you have experienced. I have told you what it is not, and I have told you what it is. The Collaboration Movement is change (a reformation) that is already happening; you cannot stop it even if you wanted to.

At the turn of the 20th century, transportation options were to take a horse and buggy or walk. People in the buggy whip business were thriving. Almost overnight, the automobile replaced the horse and buggy. Those in the buggy whip business saw their businesses close due to that reformation, unless however, those business owners realized they were in the transportation business evolved with the change. They succeeded.

Change is here, the old system based in an industrial paradigm is dead and dying. Like the dinosaurs, it will soon pass from existence. The new paradigm is here. We are changing to a technology-based, open, pro-rata sharing where individuals are freed from the employee shackles and are released to become who they were made to be. If you haven't already noticed, it will be like buying a new car. You did not see many of them until you bought yours now they seem to be everywhere, especially the color you bought. You will hear collaborate this and collaborate that. It is in our advertising; it is in our news; it is in our daily language. You may as well embrace it, the reformation is here!

What was needed is a governance model, a new way to organize it. I pray I have accomplished that here. My firm, SPECTRUM Advanced Markets, Inc. on the for-profit side and Global Stewards Initiative on the non-profit side will be providing professional business advice and developing tools to users in the new Collabortist economy. Write the answers to the following questions in your journal – don't give up now you are almost done.

The questions are:
- What about You?
- Are you embracing the Reformation/Change?
- Will you engage?
- Will you establish your unique Drop qualities?
- Will you align with others into Streams?
- Will you collaborate and become powerful Rivers?
- Will you create EcoSystems and become Oceans?
- Will you emerge as a leader in the movement?
- Will you fight for your individual rights?
- Will you collaborate?
- Will you start your own personal business?
- Will you commit to share pro-rata with others?
- Will you apply the Principles of Collaborative Commonwealth™ to your life, government, society, commerce, and in your business?
- Will you interface and connect with others?
- Will you explore a new resume so the economy can find you?

- Will you explore connecting with a CVES and valuing your intangible and tangible assets for multiplication in the new economy?
- Will you in an open-handed way connect with people, systems, structures, networks, EcoSystems, and EcoSpheres to cause this movement to advance?
- Will you take an honest look at yourself and others and assess sound alignments, do it with honor, and play your role?

Or will you be complacent, unwilling to change, a distraction, dependent, and left behind?

This is the moral question of this book; I trust it has been an eye-opening experience. If the book has stimulated you, seek your role in the new economy and governance. **Remember, this is just the beginning our future is before us!**

Remember CollaborateUSA.com

- Please join the discussion there, ask your friends to get involved.
- We plan to also offer other resources there, so as you find them, please share what you have found.
- If you are bold, make a Facebook® post
- Make a post on Twitter®
- Or any other favorites social media – Let's get the word out!

Dr. Robert A. Needham

Thought Mastery

Have you made journal entries from each chapter in a notebook where you can reflect on the concepts and thoughts you have had since you began this book? If not, I encourage you to re-read each chapter's Thought Mastery and do the homework. You can also find the summary at chapter 12.

Take the time to answer all the questions in detail in your journal from this chapter.

Chapter 12 – Thought Leadership For A New Economy

Twelve (12) is the number of completed government. It also represents a completed cycle of experience. So when, I structured this book, I believed 12 chapters was the right amount.

I believe that Collaborative Commonwealth™ is the completed integration of man's development of social contract theory to-date. However, it is iterative; meaning we should revisit often its concepts and principles and when a new and better approach is found, integrate it into society. It is therefore dynamic and not static. This makes sense since it is Agile and not Fragile.

For simplicity and continuity, I have provided the Thought Mastery from each of the previous 11 chapters into this one chapter as a quick reference of the concepts and principles covered in this book. I have bolded key phrases, concepts and thoughts. Together with your journal, that I asked you to keep, this will be a handy reference as you implement your collaborative strategy and become a Collaboratist.

Again, I purposely kept this book tight and as few pages as possible to convey this Collaborative Movement. There will be much more as our website, a work in progress, matures and all the elements of this vision unfold.

The website is: **www.CollaborateUSA.com**

Thought Mastery: Chapter 1

You are a unique Drop. With whom can you align to form a Stream? Will you become a Stream-Builder? What like interests can make your dreams come true as you merge with others to form Streams and ultimately become a River? Do you have the vision to merge with other Rivers to become your own Ocean? Like Phil Robertson, what is your one BIG Idea?

Remember at each level of collaboration, there are new multiplied marketplaces each one offering an abundance of wealth that can be harvested. Do not rush the process. Take each opportunity as it comes and don't jump ahead of the timing. Build on your sequential successes. **Collaborate more than compete with others and merge your ideas with theirs**.

170

In the next chapter we will learn about *Leadership Emergence* and how that can impact your future. By the time you fully understand the unique difference between Collaborative Commonwealth™ and the broken capitalistic or socialistic *hierarchal system* (which is failing this planet) you will be armed with the tools to harvest your own success.

What are you called or inspired to do? What is your purpose? The best is yet to come if we learn to collaborate the Drops into mighty Oceans which maintain the identity of each Drop and learn to pro-rata share the profits according to one's labor; not hoard them into broken economic and governmental systems based in hierarchical systems of *top down leadership;* but into collaborative systems where we are all *working together for the common good and each is properly rewarded for their contribution.*

Thought Mastery: Chapter 2

In your journal, list all the ways you have intentionally or unintentionally begun to emerge as a leader. Then write answers for each of the questions that follow.

- Where are you in your LET Phases?
- Are you now in Convergence?
- What are you doing to establish spheres of influence?
- How have you invested in yourself to become a more effective leader?
- Which characteristics of effective leadership do you have?

- What outside influences could take you to the next level if you approach with an open mind as to what others have to say and offer?
- Are you maximizing your potential?
- Have you found your first followers?
- Do you treat your followers as equals?
- Do you pro-rata share with your followers according to their commitment of time, talent, and treasure.
- Where is your Ocean?
- Are you willing to become a *"Blue Ocean Captain?"*

In the next chapter, we will begin to learn how to govern, control, steward, and manage our calling (Purpose). This is called *"Governance."*

Thought Mastery: Chapter 3

What do you see as the processes of CHANGE going on right now?

Do you understand the concept of hegemony? As our nation, like Rome, deploys its military around the world and continues to increase entitlement programs, do you believe that the United States will continue to be a global hegemon? If not, what impact will this change have on your way of life in the 21st century?

Collaboration is emerging as a new social contract theory (see chapter 7 for more detail) in the 21st century which I propose we should use Collaborative Commonwealth™ as its form of governance, creating Collaboratists who believe in pro-rata sharing and caring for their community and nation.

Dee Hock...*"the organization of the future will be the embodiment of community based on a 'shared purpose'... Purpose first, then proceeds to Principles, People, and Concept; and only then to Structure and Practice..."*

There are cycles of approximately 250 years, (hegemony – revolution – independence) which cause *"power to move from the hands of a few to the hands of many"* and back again. The Industrial Revolution took back our power and placed it in the hands of new kings, the capitalist corporations, headed by Imperial CEOs. **We are not saying corporations are bad, but that their governance has to REFORM.**

Collaborative Commonwealth™ is more like:
- A Republic or Commonwealth
- A Confederation
- A Reformation
- Believes in Pro-Rata Sharing and Community Caring

Collaborative Commonwealth™ is NOT:
- A Democracy (headed to Dictatorship)
- A Federation
- A Revolution
- Driven by Scarcity or social concepts of Free or Entitlement.

With Collaborative Commonwealth™ sovereignty is at the individual level allowing voluntary participation in projects and the ability to succeed or withdraw when the plan does not meet their Purpose.

Sharing will play the major role in the emergence of the Collaborative Economy.

Technology has brought reformation (change) in the publication, photography, music, and communication. It will be a major component in how we collaborate and govern in the future.

Thought Mastery: Chapter 4

There is a need for change in how our nation governs. The chart that follows captures the issues.

Industrial Economy	Social Economy	Collaborative Economy
Centered on Accumulation of Wealth (Self)	Centered in Distribution of Wealth (Network)	Centered in Sharing Access to Wealth (EcoSystem or EcoSphere)
Self Centered or Scarcity Mindset	Free or Entitlement Mindset	Pro-Rata Share Mindset
Vertically Integrated	Horizontally Integrated	Circularly Integrated
Dictator Power At The Top	Democracy Small Group Control	Commonwealth Individual Power

You should understand the differences between a capitalist entrepreneur, a social entrepreneur, and a Collaboratist entrepreneur.

Thought Mastery: Chapter 5

De Soto..."Capital is a force that raises productivity of labor and creates the wealth of nations"... Assets must have title to become capital, if not, they are "dead capital" and unable to be multiplied into wealth and are called "extralegal."

The Collaborative Economy must develop a system to properly value tangible and intangible assets.

Currency which is based in debt (fiat) is dying and will not be sustainable.

Economic or Fiscal Slavery is when you work for your house, your food, and they pay you just enough to pay for all that.

Physical Slavery is when someone else pays for your house, etc. It is a form of entitlement.

Wealth does not come from percentage increase, but from multiplication. Do you understand the Rule of 72 and how to apply it in your life? Are you committed to "own your life" or "to rent your life out" for someone else to multiply their wealth using your talent? Write in your journal how you feel about this right now.

This book cannot render legal, accounting, or financial advice. You are encouraged to find a licensed professional to become your coach or advisor and help you with your finances.

Thought Mastery: Chapter 6

There are four principles from the story of the teacher and the student that we need to learn to Multiply and Prosper in the Collaborative Economy, and they are:

- Principle 1: The Principle of the Harvest
  - Sow with a Purpose, not into Chaos.
  - Don't scatter your seed greater than you can plow.
  - Always plant more than you need.
  - From one seed, you can feed a nation.

- Principle 2: If You Don't Take A Risk, You Won't Multiply.

- Principle 3: The Principle of Excess – Investing with Others' Capital.

- Principle 4: The Principle of Gleaning, Sharing or Caring for Others

Principles of Collaborative Commonwealth™ I should adopt in my life are:

1. I should maintain my individual rights and values, but not become an island separate from others.

2. I should strive to collaborate with others to the pro-rata (sharing) benefit of others according to their contributions to the project.

3. As an open-handed individual, manager, or steward, I should apply The Four Principles of Multiplication to Prosper in the Collaborative Economy in my life. I can be valued (sow my seed well) by multiplying my resources to meet the needs of the collaborative group and myself. If I take investors' money, I make sure they get their money back and earn an excellent return on investment. Lastly, I must determined **how much is enough** and give generously to others in need so that I can bless them and thereby be blessed. Other-centered, not self-centered is my principle.

4. I find ways to collaborate with others and seek not to labor solely for my personal gain.

5. It takes TEAM work to make a dream work, not more of me. There is rest when I collaborate with others.

Thought Mastery: Chapter 7

With the CHANGE coming, we need reformation.

What caused the Occupy Movement to fail was a lack of Leadership Emergence. It allowed outside factions to use propaganda to pick their ideals apart.

Our current governance system is broken. We need reformation. We've got to stop the crisis of fear brought on by scarcity, and we have to control our purse strings (entitlements). You can't borrow yourself out of debt!

Social Media has proven it is the way to reach literally billions of people as in the case of Facebook®.

Any future aspect of global planning, must consider:
1) social networks/circles
2) electronic commerce, and
3) the multicultural aspects of this collaboration

The financial impact of this group uniting as a consumer organization, would control not only the majority of goods and services, but could declare its own community currency.

Translating this to a business environment, where governance is important, and there is commerce and exchange between producers and consumers. They relate through commerce, but they do not attempt to govern each other. Instead, they operate by contract (covenant or agreement) where all parties can reach "mutual assent" on how the project will be achieved and how each will be compensated according to their pro-rata value exchange. Future governance will be more virtual and operate by agreements (See chapter 8).

There will need to be created a better system. I call it the **Community Value Exchange System (CVES)**, this is were liquidity of assets takes place by establishing a currency-equivalent for each asset. A community crypto-currency (C³) may be the answer. This currency must be able to degrade so that in the event of a technology disaster where we lost connectivity or even computers, we could still provide goods and services in the local marketplace by the use of script.

Thought Mastery: Chapter 8

Are you ready to become a CHANGE AGENT?

Do you have a grasp on the 20, 40, 80, and 250 year cycles that impact our economy?

What is your plan if we have another economic crisis between 2014 and 2023. According to numerous economic experts it is not if, but when. Dent, says the economy won't recover until 2023 based on the generational spending in the 20, 40, and 80 year cycles. What is your plan? Survival or Multiplication?

Have you looked into Massive Open Online Courses (MOOCs). You may need to increase your skills in several areas, why not start today?

Do you embrace "Every Individual Will Be A Company?" If so, what is your company going to be able to contribute? Where are your fellow Streams, Rivers, or Oceans you need to connect. Have you started to create your "New Resume" for the Collaborative Economy?

Davidow, in *The Virtual Corporation,* said by 2015 the US will either be a leader in the new economy or be a postindustrial version of a developing country. How do you plan to collaborate in the future?

Do you know where you will connect, where is your Framisdortin?

It will take unity and enough social dissatisfaction with status quo to effect change. Pro-rata sharing is at the core of this concept. When we value human time, talent, and treasure (like Curiosume), exchange that value as liquid currency (like CVES), are connected by technology and agreement (like Framisdortin), and have EcoSystem Confederation (chapter 9), we will have the governance model for a new Collaborative Economic System called Collaborative Commonwealth™. It will emerge agile and ready for the next 250 year cycle of economic growth where individuals (Drops) are rewarded and valued; where products, services, concepts, can pro-rata share profits; and where EcoSystems (Oceans) can emerge and thrive.

Thought Mastery: Chapter 9

Collaborative Commonwealth™ as a form of governance is not Federal, Democratic, Capitalist, or Socialist; it is Confederate, balanced by open pro-rata sharing, and Collabortist in nature.

If you recall how often the next reformation or revolution maintains a remnant the former system; Collaborative

Commonwealth™ or the EcoSystem (economic system), does not throw out all aspects of the former economic systems. In fact, I believe we have retained the best practices of governance and embodied them into Collaborative Commonwealth™.

Confederation is not just a southern United States historical ideal; it is defined as a union, league, or alliance of sovereign units (Drops, Steams, Rivers, and Oceans) for common action in relation to other units.

This concept of revenue sharing (sometimes know as patronage) is different from commissions and share ownership.

Re-read all the quotes from Seth Godin in this chapter.

Where do you connect right now? Is it with other individuals, with systems, with structures, with networks, or with an EcoSystem? It could be multiple places. Write your thoughts in your journal.

Thought Mastery: Chapter 10

Have you decided to engage and become involved? Will you emerge as a leader?

From Assessment 1, which type are you?

From Assessment 2, What is your Meyers-Briggs ® four letter personality designation. Did you read the detailed report to understand how you work and interrelate (connect) with others? What was your DISC profile? Which did you choose StengthsFinder or The Merit Profile™? Do you know how to find others who might be a "Sound Alignment" for your team?

From Assessment 3, have you made your list of distractions? Remember to maximize your future; you must minimize your distractions.

From Assessment 4, how many holes did you have? Remember, if you don't patch the hull, you leak and your ship cannot get to its destination no matter how much wind you have in your sails.

Thought Mastery: Chapter 11

Have you made journal entries from each chapter in a notebook where you can reflect on the concepts and thoughts you have had since you began this book? If not, I encourage you to re-read each chapter's Thought Mastery and do the homework. You can also find the summary at chapter 12.

Take the time to answer all the questions in detail in your journal from this chapter.

The questions are:
- What about You?
- Are you embracing the Reformation/Change?
- Will you engage?
- Will you establish your unique Drop qualities?

- Will you align with others into Streams?
- Will you collaborate and become powerful Rivers?
- Will you create EcoSystems and become Oceans?
- Will you emerge as a leader in the movement?
- Will you fight for your individual rights?
- Will you collaborate?
- Will you start your own personal business?
- Will you commit to share pro-rata with others?
- Will you apply the Principles of Collaborative Commonwealth™ to your life, government, society, commerce, and in your business?
- Will you interface and connect with others?
- Will you explore a new resume so the economy can find you?
- Will you explore connecting with a CVES and valuing your intangible and tangible assets for multiplication in the new economy?
- Will you in an open-handed way connect with people, systems, structures, networks, EcoSystems, and EcoSpheres to cause this movement to advance?
- Will you take an honest look at yourself and others and assess sound alignments, do it with honor, and play your role?

Or will you be complacent, unwilling to change, a distraction, dependent, and left behind?

Final Thoughts

Collaborative Commonwealth™ is not an idea whose time is coming, the CHANGE is already here. Whether, your role is to finance the young ones, Lead your part of the movement, or simple encourage the youth to take our country back. You are needed. You are the Drop, the most important part of the system, the foundation, without your independence it will never be completed.

I pray you will engage and together we set the course of destiny and CHANGE the world. Its going to CHANGE with or without us, I just think we should guide it to a better way.

THE BEGINNING

NOTES

Made in the USA
Charleston, SC
09 March 2015